Beyond Victimhood

Embrace the Future

by
Tom Fitzgerald

Published by Fairview Press, 2450 Riverside Avenue South, Minneapolis MN 55454.

Library of Congress Cataloging-in-Publication Data

Fitzgerald, Tom.
      Beyond victimhood : embrace the future / by Tom Fitzgerald,
        p.   cm.
      ISBN 0-925190-42-X : $10.95
      1. Adjustment (Psychology) 2. Psychic trauma. 3. Victims--
Psychology. 4. Self-defeating behavior. I. Title.
      BF335.4.F58 1995
      362.82'4--dc20

First printing: February 1995

Printed in the United States of America

99 98 97 96 95   7 6 5 4 3 2 1

Designed by Circus Design
Cover photography by R. Wahlstrom, The Image Bank

Publisher's Note: Fairview Press publishes books and other materials related to the subjects of physical health, mental health, and chemical dependency. Its publications, including *Beyond Victimhood*, do not necessarily reflect the philosophy of Fairview Hospital and Healthcare Services or their treatment programs

Sweet child, it is not the expert or the philosopher or the self-anointed one who brings you the truth about happiness, for this truth, the most ancient of all wisdoms, is not channeled to the few; it is embedded in the many. It is inscribed within the sacred tabernacle of every human soul. At most, you need only be reminded of what you already know. Listen therefore not to the words that fill your ears but to the resonance that fills your heart.
—Mother

*This book is respectfully dedicated to
the true heroes in this world;
Those who build of self by giving of self*

*And to my father
with whom I got even
By getting on with it*

Contents

Foreword

In 1342, Thomas Aquinas, in creating his list of basic human emotions, listed hope, a singular appearance of a much-needed feeling. Tom Fitzgerald has written a book offering us hope.

Poignant, personal, filled with wisdom, well-written, and readable describes the style and content; but how does one describe walking outside on the first warm, sun-filled day of spring? *Beyond Victimhood* moves the sun-warmth inside, to the core of our need. The path of spirituality it forges is not backward but forward, to the soul-awakening and inspiring journey of a spiritual life.

The healing offered is intergenerational, societal, and planetary, but the wound and the medicine are deeply personal, allowing us to embrace both our shared wisdom and the unique, instinctive guides so many of us have lost contact with. This book is one of connecting and belonging.

Beyond Victimhood supports our personal belief system of recovery and complements the philosophy of our professional work offered in our LifeWorks and Life Balance programs. We believe the reason to go back and look at the past is to connect it to how we reenact or react to our past in our present.

The future of the world does not lie in the hands of children. The future of the world lies in the hands that hold the hands of children, and we cannot hold the hands of children until we hold the hands and heal the hearts of our own childness.

Beyond Victimhood is an insightful and helpful guide for this healing journey.

—*Terry Kellogg*, C.C.P.D.
—*Marvel Harrison*, Ph.D.

Acknowledgments

The author wishes to express his deep appreciation to the following people for their unconditional contributions to this book: Pam Lessard, Sally and Bruce Simson, Mary Remick, and Shirley Walker, for having the courage to accept gifts from a stranger; Ray Goodwin, for his faith and trust; Jack Caravela, without whose encouragement this book would never have been written; Laurie and Josh, for their thorough critiques and many savvy suggestions; Laurie again, for the countless enlightenments and insights; Melissa Osborne, for reviewing the manuscript; Will Conway, for critiquing the front matter; Paul Wolfe, for the many priceless hours of soulful conversation; Al Zuckerman, for his faith and wise counsel; Ed Wedman, for his faith and seemingly infinite patience; Jay Hanson, for his editorial magic; and Gil Goodgion, for teaching me to look for the *real* problem before attempting to solve what appeared to be the problem.

Special thanks to Terry Kellogg, C.C.P.D., Marvel Harrison, Ph.D., and Bernie S. Siegel, M.D., for their unconditional generosity. And to *you*, dear reader, for listening.

Preface:
A Note from Son Josh

Dear Pop,

I am honored to be asked to write the Preface; the book, containing both of our thoughts, both of our souls—is a symbol for the end of a painful, frustrating era in both our lives. We're collaborating now, not fighting, not tearing each other down. It feels good. I'm not out of the woods yet; I still kick kitchen cupboards to pieces and I still rage at myself on occasion for being a stupid buffoon with absolutely no redeeming qualities, but the episodes are far more rare and the demons' voices are growing weaker. And, like last night, I still sometimes have dreams about you criticizing me and lecturing me and making me feel small. But the worst is over for me, and, I suspect, for you too. The book tells me so. I can feel *it.*

While reading my father's book, I could not help but think about the broader implications of his essential message: that within each of us lies the strength, the power, the raw materials with which to build a happy, fulfilling life. For while my father addresses primarily individuals who were traumatized as children by dysfunctional parents, the message holds true for groups of people, such as blacks, Jews, women, and native Americans who have been the victims, and continue to be victims, of social injustice.

It is, to say the least, a troubled world. Every day, images of agonized faces confront me on my television screen, their cries rattling my heart in its comfortable environs. The suffering is great, and so little ever seems to be done to stop the tragedy.

Sadly, though, the oppressed seem too often to become consumed by their anger and frustration. Their hearts fill with bitterness, their words fill with a searing rage that is more likely to foster fear or contempt in the oppressor than compassion or shame. And worse, the anger and frustration can explode into self-destructive violence.

While I certainly feel that anger and frustration are natural emotions to be invoked in those who have been injured or abused, there comes a time when the victim must decide that, regardless of what happens, they will no longer allow themselves to be tormented by their circumstance. The irony is that by allowing oneself to become so enraged, and by looking too much for the oppressor to right the wrongs, the victim continues to place the oppressor in the position of power and control.

Regardless of how social reform efforts are proceeding, victims of oppression have to realize that the power to be happy and healthy and vital lies WITHIN them, not in the law of the land or in the attitude of the oppressor. To look outward for peace is to open oneself to frustration and despair. Most importantly for those who have been beaten down by the cruelty and indifference of others, who have perhaps come to believe that the prejudices about them are true, is the understanding that self-empowerment comes with healing and nurturing the spirit. You need no one else to green your garden, least of all your tormentor, and the steps you take along this path become the lessons you must learn: that you are inherently worthy, that you are a miracle, that you have incalculable strength that dwarfs the political, economic and psychological power wielded by every bully that has ever scourged the face of the earth.

This philosophy of self-healing and self-empowerment stands independent of questions of social justice and cultural reform. Of course we all must strive to make this a healthier world in which to live. But do not think that even if by some miracle the injustices were to end tomorrow, the hurt inside will simply go away. The healing process must be pursued separately, regardless of what the victimizers ultimately choose to do.

It is, for me, the ultimate liberation, the ultimate sense of empowerment, to know, and FEEL that I can choose to heal myself, and to not allow others to plant weeds in my spiritual garden. They can break my bones, they can hurl endless blasts of verbal cruelty at me, but if I choose not to listen, if I have discovered my own essential worth, if I am being who I really need to be, then amidst all the horrors I can always find the strength to smile, and it is as sunshine pouring down on that most essential garden, the Garden Within.

—*Josh Fitzgerald*
Bryn Mawr, Pennsylvania

Introduction

In recent years, countless numbers of us who have experienced some form of life-altering trauma in our lives have become aware of why we are always so filled with pain and anger, so crippled by despair and self-loathing, so hopelessly isolated and alone—so irredeemably "different." Finally, we were given a label for our anguish and with it, a pathology. We were victims. We were victims of parental dysfunction; we were victims of incest or sexual abuse; we were victims of emotional exploition or physical predation; we were victims of systematic or incidental violence; we were victims of neglect or indifference; we were victims of humiliation or intolerance; we were victims of betrayal.

Our eyes finally opened, some of us eventually found our way into one or more of the various recovery programs (see *Glossary*) that purport to accommodate the special needs of victims: twelve-step programs, individual or group psychotherapy, therapeutic massage, Eye Movement Desensitization and Reprocessing Therapy, A Course in Miracles, Gigong, and so forth. Others of us, however, chose simply to close our eyes again, finding the light of our new awareness perhaps a little too bright to bear.

Those of us who have chosen to keep our eyes shut have continued, of course, to be still wounded, and therefore still wounding, for one cannot remain wounded, either in psyche or in soul, without passing on one's woundedness. However, even those of us who have passed through one or more recovery programs have found ourselves to be still wounded, either in whole or in part. Indeed, many of us find ourselves to be suffering a sort of lingering angst, emanating from deep within, like the dull, pulsating pangs from an abscessed tooth—or from a deep, unattended hunger.

An Incomplete Recovery

The reason for this lingering angst is that many traditional recovery programs only go so far. They give us permission to stop viewing ourselves as inherently flawed or lacking and to start viewing ourselves as innocent victims of some form of debilitating trauma. And they give us permission to begin to heal ourselves—to begin to take care of our wounded child within (see *Glossary*). However, most of these programs do not advocate, at least not strongly enough, moving beyond the self-preoccupation that seems to be an essential part of every recovery process, but that should never be allowed to become either its accidental result or its intentional goal.

In other words, these programs give permission for us to move our "secular" center—to make what academics would call First Order changes (changes in surface behavior, job, friends, spouse, home, geographical location, wardrobe, body type). However, they fail to sufficiently address our need to move our spiritual (ego-transcending) center (see *Glossary*)—to make Second Order changes in our beliefs and our behavior. Or they address this latter need in a way that is not readily accessible to many of us, such as in narrowly religious terms or in fuzzy, elusive New Agey terms. The result is too often a recursive, self-perpetuating condition in which we become increasingly self-absorbed and more and more mired in the muck of victimhood (see *Glossary*). We tend to spend more time grieving over and attempting to recover treasures forever lost than in seeking the treasures still open to us.

The fundamental problem with many recovery programs is that their underlying philosophies do not sufficiently acknowledge that all true and lasting recovery from deep physical and emotional woundings must be realized primarily at the spiritual level. In other words, whatever recovery path we choose or are asked to follow, it must ultimately lead us away from defining our essential needs exclusively in terms of secular principles ("If I change my job, home, spouse, body, hairdresser et al, then everything will be OK"), and more toward defining our essential needs in terms of such ego-transcending principles as: We make a real difference in our own lives when we strive to make a real difference in the lives of others.

This problem is greatly exacerbated by a Puritan-based culture that has ironically become much more comfortable talking about condoms and penises than about "soul" and spirituality, and that traditionally has held very limited notions about what spirituality is and what role it plays in the human experience. To appreciate the possible effects of such limited notions, consider the impact on one's overall world view of the following possible insight into the nature of spirituality: *Religion is a room with a door; spirituality is everything else.*

An Offering

This book offers a process for moving our spiritual center down our own chosen path, at our own pace.

The process offered consists of four general tasks that ask us to make peace with the past, so we can let go of it; to make peace with ourselves, so we can "deserve" a better fate; to rewrite the old, unchallenged scripts that no longer work for us, so we can take real control over our own life; and to discover who we really are, so we can be who we really are.

This book does not so much offer new truths (see *Glossary*) as it simply reminds us of what we already know. It does not so much provide parched lips with cool water as it lends a hand with the ancient pump to which we all have equal access. Its expertise is our expertise; its wisdom, our wisdom.

Each of us knows where we are; each of us knows where we need to go. The purpose of this guide book is simply to help us choose the path that best accommodates our particular situation; to nudge us on our way; and to help us use our own considerable wits to get past all the traps and obstacles that inevitably will attempt to thwart our progress.

This book is ultimately a journey of the whole self, along a path uniquely of our own choosing. The specific guidance offered in this book, joined with the will to make real changes—at the most fundamental level of our being—is all any of us needs to move beyond our woundedness to become the whole, unconditionally loving, ultimately fulfilled human beings each of us was meant to be.

There is still time.

In fact, time is not really a problem, is it?

Each of us has all the time there is.

Zen & the Art of Relationship Maintenance

In the popular cult novel *Zen and the Art of Motorcycle Maintenance*, the narrator goes on a cross-country quest with his young son, riding a motorcycle. The purpose of the narrator's quest is to find both "real meaning", in the form of Quality (as exemplified by first-rate motorcycle maintenance), and the narrator's "true self" (as symbolized by a phantom the narrator refers to as Phaedrus). The premise under which the narrator is operating appears to be that real meaning is something one can only find by pursuing some kind of largely intellectual quest.

Since reading this strangely-compelling book, I have often wondered what would have happened had the narrator simply parked his motorcycle by the side of the road, turned to his young son riding on the back, and given him a big squeeze: the I-unconditionally-accept-you hug that represented what the narrator himself needed, both to receive and to give. My sense is that the narrator would not have needed to venture any further into the heart of his own darkness, that in turning to his son, to healing his relationship with his son, which was obviously in need of healing, he would have freed himself from the gravitational pull of what had, for him, become a black hole within, an anguished ego turned recursively in on itself.

Indeed, the "meaning" the narrator was so fiercely seeking seemed to be right under his nose all along. Instead of being embodied in motorcycle maintenance or in the elusive Phaedrus', it lay instead in the quality of his relationships—and especially in the quality of his relationship with his own son. The narrator was on an exclusively intellectual quest when what he actually needed to be on was a largely spiritual quest—not, as Emily Dickinson has taught us, pursued on some exotic, quixotic road to Damascus, but in one's own back yard.

If you are at least open to this same notion, you will likely find what is offered within the following pages of at least some value. If not, no harm done. As you make your assessment, though, please keep in mind that this book is not an all-or-nothing proposition. You can take what feels comfortable in the moment and leave the rest. If you wish to, you can always come back for the rest later.

Speaking the Same Language

All communication is imperfect. Much of the meaning (thoughts, ideas, observations, feelings) we intend to communicate to others is either distorted or lost outright at some fateful point between original intent and final interpretation. Witness the amount of misunderstanding that takes place every day—every moment!—between parents and children, bosses and subordinates, sacred texts and truth seekers, legal documents and lay persons, newspapers and readers, teachers and pupils, men and women.

"What we have here is a failure to communicate."

Many forces can conspire against precision in human communication, including the deliberate attempts to mislead or obfuscate that have become so common in advertising and politics today, and so heavily emulated elsewhere. One of the more prevalent of the benign forces conspiring against accuracy in communication, however, concerns the very nature of language itself: Words, of their very nature, are inadequate vessels to hold perfect meaning. They leak. They leave puddles (not to mention muddles). For example, what does "love" mean in the commandment "Love thy neighbor as thy self?" Indeed, what does "neighbor" mean? In fact, what does neighbor mean all by itself? Where does neighbor leave off and stranger begin?

In truth, neighbor is really a continuum of possible points of meaning, just as love is. However, we humans are not able to deal with this kind of reality, at least not very efficiently, so we must invent a reality that we can deal with. Therefore, we arbitrarily assign global labels to various whole categories or continua, such as love, hate, neighbor, stranger. Then, as we need to, we break these whole categories down into subcategories, such as parental love, romantic love, spiritual love, puppy love. No matter how many categories or subcategories we arbitrarily invent, however, none of these enjoys a precise boundary that perfectly distinguishes it from all others. There is always an element of blurring, of imprecision, and therefore always a lack of agreement on the precise meaning of terms whenever a sender attempts to communicate with a receiver.

Complicating matters is the "individualized" meaning, or connotation, that each of us brings to any particular term. This level of meaning is the unique flavorings each of us adds to the raw batter (dictionary meaning) of a term. For example, the term "honor" in the commandment "Honor thy father and thy mother" may mean one thing to a fifteen-year-old girl brought up by two loving, respectful, validating parents; quite another to a fifteen-year-old girl being sexually abused by her father while her mother appears not to notice.

Despite all the forces working against us, however, we can lessen the possibility of miscommunicating by making at least some effort to clarify how certain key terms are intended to be interpreted within a particular context. Take, for example, the two terms we discussed earlier from the commandment "Love thy neighbor as thy self." It would have helped us all immeasurably if the author of this ancient text had expressed his intent in a little more detail; if he had, for example, added a simple footnote that provided us with valuable information on his precise intent without detracting from the poetic and rhetorical aesthetics that were likely as much of his purpose as imparting moral guidance: Love in this context means to honor the miracle of being shared by all living things. Neighbor means everyone and everything with whom and with which we share the common miracle of being.

In the interests of establishing the precise meaning of certain key terms used in this guide book, you will be referred, as appropriate, to the glossary located at the end of this book. I know—being asked to break your concentration to pump a little (hot?) air into a word is a little like being called to the phone during your favorite TV program. I sympathize. However, you are strongly encouraged to do it anyway. What's being "sold" here just might be worth the interruption.

A Note to Survivors

Certain exercises in this guide ask the reader to recall events that may be a source of intense feelings—not only the pain, anger, and grief likely to be triggered by images of injury, betrayal, or loss, but also the shame and guilt (see *Glossary*) we are likely to experience if we are self-blaming in regard to certain events in our past. In cases where such feelings are likely—or even just possibly—to be particularly intense, or particularly confusing, they should not be dealt with in isolation.

If you are a survivor of incest or other sexual abuse, therefore—or if you otherwise feel you may be particularly vulnerable to the effects of recalling highly disturbing events from your past—you are strongly advised to seek the advice of a licensed, reputable therapist before you engage in any activities—those in this or any other guide—that are likely to trigger an intense emotional response. If you are not currently under the care of such a therapist, you may wish to refer to Appendix C in this guide for help in finding one.

***

The author of this book is a fellow traveler who was headed down a path of despair and self-destruction until he was able to recognize the simple, sometimes hard truths that are the basis of this book. For him, the process of change he built around these truths was ultimately a soul saver—not only for himself but for others in his life as well. For you, they can be whatever you want them to be. You are the pilot of your own ship.

Bon voyage!

—Tom Fitzgerald

Who Are We?

Whenever we are with people, even people with whom we are familiar, we feel different; we feel we do not belong. We feel anxious and uncomfortable.

Who are we?

In our family of origin, some of us assumed the role of parent and peacemaker. We became a responsible adult before we had a chance to be a carefree child. We now grieve for what has been irretrievably lost.

Who are we?

We do not know what normal is—how to act the part, even what lines to say—though we sense it when we see it in others. We are forever self-conscious in costumes that never quite fit.

Who are we?

We tend to be either super responsible or super irresponsible. Either we try to do it all, or we avoid doing anything at all.

Who are we?

Authority figures diminish us; they make us feel anxious and vulnerable. We may wrestle them to the floor in fantasy, but only to quake and grovel before them at our very next encounter.

Who are we?

We have a compulsive need to be in control. Control is four walls and a moat.

Who are we?

If we succeed, it was because we were lucky. If we fail, it was because we didn't try quite hard enough. We know if we try just a little harder, though, eventually we'll get it right.

Who are we?

We tend to get hooked—if not on one of the Big Three (alcohol, tobacco, or drugs), then likely on food, power, work, sex, achievement, crises, or gambling. We even get hooked on others who get hooked.

Who are we?

Some of us have come to identify ourselves as Victim. Some of us begin each day by pinning a large Purple Heart directly to our bleeding flesh.

Who are we?

We tend to be rescuers—case workers, volunteers, nurses, therapists, clergy, teachers, protesters, super moms, bleeding hearts. If the world is to be saved from injustice and travail, we are the ones who will do it or utterly exhaust ourselves in the trying.

Who are we?

We are anxious most of the time, even when alone. For us, anxiety is normalcy. Anxiety is something about to happen, something left undone, something not yet perfected, something not yet under our control.

Who are we?

We tend to take life very seriously, too seriously to engage in any kind spontaneous frivolity or play for the pure fun of it. Fun is a reward we plan (unto death) for others, not something we give to ourselves.

Who are we?

It is difficult for us to invest trust, almost impossible for us to risk intimacy. For us, trust and intimacy are the same wolf of betrayal wearing the clothing of the sheep and the lamb.

Who are we?

We tend to think in terms of all or nothing. If we can't do it all, understand it all, achieve it all, be it all, have it all—if we can't be perfect—we fail. We fail a lot.

Who are we?

We tend to yo-yo between extremes. One moment we are all-powerful, wholly in control, fiercely independent, needful of no one; the next we are pathetically powerless, clingingly dependent, worthless, and ashamed. Beneath it all, we are isolated and alone—self-enslaved in our own private little agony.

Who are we?

We once promised ourselves we would never be like the parents who wounded us in some deeply felt way. Now well into our own adulthood, we have yet to allow ourselves to see the full reality of what we have since become.

Who are we?

People are always blaming their circumstances for what they are. I don't believe in circumstances. The people who get on in this world are the people who get up and look for the circumstances they want, and, if they can't find them, make them.
—George Bernard Shaw

At times most of us quarrel with our fate: If only I were more intelligent, more successful, more assertive. If only my parents had been more loving. But this is a loss of time, a loss of energy, a loss of happiness. It is senseless, because fate is not subject to negotiation. Its "givenness" is total.

But that is only half the story. For the total "givenness" of our fate is matched by the total freedom we have to react to our fate. It is as if we were dealt a hand of cards. Once we have them, we are free to play them as we choose.
—G. Peter Fleck
Come As You Are

The Buddha of PBS:
Context and Conditional Love

We must see the need for achieving spiritual, unconditional love as a
means of healing ourselves and our fellow travelers on this planet.
—Bernie S. Siegel, M.D.

Context is everything. Context is our universe, our environment, our culture, our home, our relationships, our DNA, our gender, our health, our sexual orientation, our knowledge, our values, our presence in the moment. Context is our belief system and all the forces and influences that have played a role in forming and shaping that system—including key persons in our lives who have instilled our most fundamental beliefs about ourselves, about our reason for being here, and about the tone and tenor of the world in which we live.

For any particular one of us, these fundamental beliefs about ourselves and our world are not so much a function of the tall standing truths (see *Glossary*) or deep mother lodes of logic to which we all have access. Rather, they are a function of the extent to which the primary nurturers and shapers in our lives loved and validated us when we were yet squishy clay in their hands. Did they love us unconditionally? Did they consistently and persistently remind us, in word and in deed, we were of absolute, undiminishable worth? Did they treat us with the same respect and dignity they required or wished for themselves? Or did they love us only to the extent we were pleasing to them? Conforming to them. Not a burden to them? Did they perhaps withhold their love from us altogether?

1

As I Believe, Thus I Am

As cognitive, largely self-defining, willful creatures, we are what we believe, we do what we believe. Indeed:

- If we believe we are responsible for everybody else's happiness, we will tend to be overly involved in the lives of others, and under-involved in our own life.

- If we believe we must control all the events within our immediate environment in order to be safe, we will tend to be directive and rigid.

- If we believe we must earn our way to the affections of others, we will tend to be what we think others want us to be rather than who we were intended to be.

- If we believe that numbing out is the only way we can ever escape the relentless ache in our soul, we will tend to be addictive and self-destructive.

- If we believe we will find lasting peace only through "justice," we will tend to be more concerned with getting even than with 'getting on with it."

- If we believe we are too victimized to even begin to repair all the damage, we will tend to wait to be rescued.

Up to a point, we can attribute what we believe, and therefore what we have become, to the influences of powerful agents and forces—visible and invisible—outside ourselves: family legacy, religious teachings, cultural norms, accidental circumstances. We can even choose not to attribute our beliefs at all, preferring instead to float innocently on the mere surface of the great ocean of our reality.

There comes a time, however—no one can ever tell us exactly when this moment arrives, only that it does indeed arrive—there comes a time when all that we believe (or disbelieve), all that we are (or are not), and all that we do (or fail to do) becomes a choice. There comes a time when the myriad of contexts that define who and what we are cease to be the absolute monarchs of our fate and become nothing more (or less) than the hues on the palette of possibilities from which we paint the portrait of our own life, our own fate. There comes a time when the sum total of all our woes and wounds becomes a magnificent opportunity for us, as willful, self-aware, self-defining, self-actualizing creatures, to "get on with it."

'Just the Way You Are'

A resonance within tells us Fred Rogers, the maternal patriarch of *Mister Rogers' Neighborhood*, has it exactly right: More than anything else, what we all need to hear, as children, as adults, as human beings, is the message Mister Rogers repeats, while looking each of us straight in the eye, during each of his programs: "I like you just the way you are." He does not echo what so many other life-shaping authorities tell us: "Be who I want you to be, *then* I will love you." He says the very opposite: "I accept the uniqueness of your individual self just as fate has ordained it. I have no need for you to be anything other than what you are. You are inherently and undiminishably *good* . . . inherently and undiminishably *worthy* . . . inherently and undiminishably *lovable*."

In emphasizing and repeating his powerful message, Mister Rogers fortifies the self-esteem (see *Glossary*) of children in the only way it can be. At the same time, he reminds us adults that if children are to be launched into this world with a belief system that will allow them to be who they were uniquely meant to be—that will empower them to steer themselves consistently in the right direction—they must grow, develop, and unfold in a context of love and acceptance that is innocent of all guile, steadfastly unambiguous, absolutely and steadfastly unconditional. Should they, or we, grow up in any other context— believing, for example, they are deserving of love and protection only to the degree they meet certain (often impossible) standards or conditions—they are almost certain to end up seeing themselves in the same mirror we likely found ourselves peering into when we read the verses of *"Who Are We?"* They are likely to end up, in other words, being distorted caricatures of who they were intended to be.

For Whom the Bell Tolls

The degree to which we see our image reflected in the verses of *"Who Are We?"* depends on the degree to which we have been shaped by conditional love (including withheld or negative love) or by personal trauma. Some of us may see ourselves so clearly, so intensely, we must look away, our reaction being like that of the hapless shopper who, bearing the accumulated burden of too many bags of potato chips, is suddenly confronted by one of those unforgiving mirrors that inexplicably adorn almost every department-store changing room. Others might see themselves as when middle-aged adults peruse old photo albums, that is, with varying degrees of discomfort and denial: "My God, that isn't me, is it? *Can't* be!"

Few of us are likely to come away from these verses without feeling at least some palpable twinge of recognition., because few of us are likely to have survived our formative years wholly untouched by the hand of conditional love or personal trauma. Even if we were blessed with parents who steadfastly refused to mold us with this powerful instrument of manipulation and control, we likely did not escape the squeeze and pull of other fingers, both visible and invisible. Indeed, the hand of conditional love can take many forms:

- If you obey the "father," you will go to heaven. If you disobey the "father," you will burn in hellfire for all eternity.

- If you drive this car, you will get all the attention you didn't get as a child. If you drive any other car, you risk even further alienation.

- If you look like the model in this ad, you will get the mate of your dreams. If you continue to look as you do now, you will get exactly what you deserve.

- If you tell us what we want to hear, we will elect you. If you tell us the truth as you see it, we will cast you out.

If we were to plot on a graph the degree to which we had been affected by the emotional and spiritual (see *Glossary*) effects of conditional love or personal trauma, the locus of our collective angst would likely form a bell-shaped curve. Those suffering only average angst would form the center of the bell-shaped curve. Those suffering more severely would form the right half of the bell, with the mostly severely affected forming the outer lip of the curve.

Please take a moment now to consider where your own experience of gnawing, soul-deep angst (unresolved grief, rage, despair, emptiness, anxiety) places you on this curve. Does your experience place you in the half of relative comfort and ease to the left? Or does it place you somewhere in the opposite half, perhaps even toward the outer lip?

In other words, where does the bell toll for thee?

Three-Headed Monster

Conditional love is a monster of three heads: It is an instrument for controlling and manipulating—of imposing one's conscious or derived will; it is an instrument for inflicting pain—for punishing, for exacting revenge or "justice"; and it is an instrument for passing an accumulated legacy of dysfunction—for doing unto others as was done unto us.

Conditional love is so potentially damaging and devastating because our need for what it denies us—unconditional acceptance, validation, and reassurance—is so very great. Conditional or withheld love is perceived and internalized as punishment at best, as abandonment or outright rejection at worst. It tells us we have failed to measure up to the expectations of those we depend on to make us feel safe and protected; it tells us we have fallen short of earning our way into the esteem of those we depend on to make us feel significant and validated; it tells us we are not deserving of the love of those we depend on to make us feel accepted and worthy. It tells us we are lacking; it tells us we are deficient; it tells us we deserve whatever pain and anxiety might be inflicted on us. Sometimes it even tells us we should not even have been born.

Conditional or withheld love spans the same continuum of intensity as does the overall effect it ultimately has on our beliefs about ourselves. Consider the following gradations (or should we say, "degradations"?):

- Being given the "silent treatment," that is, ignored to the extent we are not even there

- Being pressured to play a sport you do not wish to play

- Never being complimented for a good job or told you are loved

- Being inflicted with black-and-blue marks for breaking Grandmother's "priceless" blue vase

- Being verbally abused for being "so goddamned stupid"

- Being rejected or abandoned (emotionally and/or physically) by one parent or both

- Being sexually exploited

Our place on the curve that reflects the cumulative effects of these and other forms of conditional love and personal trauma depends on the overall intensity of our experience. To remind yourself of just how intense your own experience has been, consider the following situation:

You are in a room watching television with your father or mother, or with some other key person in your life—you choose. For the moment, please allow me to be the person you choose.

We are sitting together but apart. The mesmerizing flickerings of artificial light from the television are soothing you into a blessed numbness.

With the usual grunt, heard but not noticed, I rise from where I have been sitting. Instead of going into the kitchen, however, to get yet another snack, I step up to the pedestaled television and turn it off.

Silence.

The shade-drawn darkness closes in around you.

Moving from window to window, I draw up all the shades, pull back all the curtains, throw open all the windows. A flood of sunlight at first stings, then soothes your eyes. You feel whispers of sweet-scented air eddy playfully over your face. The disembodied voices from the television are replaced by a hubbub of bird chatter. Moving a small chair from one corner of the room, where it has perhaps not been used in years, I place it on the floor directly in front of you. Sitting down in it, facing you, I lean toward you and take both of your hands in mine. Looking straight into your eyes, I say these words:

"You are my poem, my creation, my art. You are in my image, yet you are uniquely your own self in all the universe. You have a soul, an essence, that is at once a declaration of individuality, of separateness, and at the same time a seamless connection with something boundless and eternal. I unconditionally respect the sovereignty of your separateness, the essential significance of your unbounded soul. I unconditionally give you permission to be who you are, to find your own path.

"There is nothing you could be or fail to become, nothing you could say or fail to declare, nothing you could do or fail to achieve, that could ever cause me to reject you, could ever cause me to abandon you, could ever cause me to cease loving you. Wherever you are, there is my heart, my thoughts; whenever you are in need, there is my hand, my life. You are everything you will ever need to be. You are part of the miracle; you are the miracle. I bask in the soft light that radiates from the divine ember glowing in your separate but inseparable soul. I love you just the way you are.

"I love you unconditionally."

Is this little fiction in fact your reality? Is it confirming and comforting? Does it warm the molasses of old memories? Or is it something else altogether? Does it awaken feelings that you much prefer to remain in a blessed slumber—of Rip Van Winkle proportions?

Does it perhaps cause you to catch the faint whisper of a familiar voice, emanating from deep within:

"Are you where you need to be?

"Is it time to get on with it?"

Getting on with It

There is a time to be a victim—early in recovery.
To stay a victim, however, is to remain in a childlike
position and never grow up.
—Kathleen R. O'Connell
Bruised by Life?

One of the problems of victims is that they tend to
define their whole personality as that of victim.
—Cloé Madanes
Sex, Love, and Violence

We are victims of neglect, of deprivation, of exploitation, of betrayal, of brutality. We are victims of bullies, of narcissists, of opportunists, of manipulators, of exploiters, of predators. We are victims of alcoholic parents, of self-absorbed parents, of negligent parents, of troubled parents, of abusive parents. Some of us were loved as children either conditionally or not at all. Some of us were neglected, even betrayed, by those on whom we were wholly dependent, or in whom we were naturally trusting. Some of us were abused physically or sexually.

We were damaged; we were diminished. We were cut, not to the quick, but to the core—the heart, the soul. We were cheated of the innocence and magic of a normal childhood; of the joy and fulfillment of a normal adulthood. We were made to feel hopelessly deficient, irredeemably unworthy.

To protect ourselves from truths we could not bear to acknowledge, we became the masons of our own reality, building walls of denial around whatever we desperately needed to hide, or to hide from. Inside these walls, we found our only sure safety. Eventually, our walls of denial began to crumble and collapse, as all walls of human design must, and we became painfully aware of the no-longer-deniable reality of our victimhood (see *Glossary*)—the debilitating degree to which we have been emotionally crippled. We now find ourselves filled with grief over what has been irretrievably lost; with ache from the relentless throb of old, unhealed wounds; with anger (see *Glossary*) and bitterness toward those who have damaged and diminished us.

We have been able to take solace, however, in acknowledging and eventually accepting that what happened to us was not *our* fault—not something we deserved because of irredeemable deficiencies or shortcomings—but simply the result of the particular victimization we suffered, as, for example, in the case of family dysfunction relentlessly and accumulatively passed down from one generation to the next. We have also taken solace in acknowledging and accepting that we are not the only ones on this planet who have spent their entire lives feeling crushingly alone and isolated—defectively "different." Indeed, there is, we now realize, a whole universe of like others out there, eager and willing to nod in knowing fraternity as we sit in the inclusive circle of our common discomfort.

Heartened by our new-found awareness and new-formed connections, we have embarked on a quest for self-empowerment and normalcy (we know it when we see it): We have read, consumed, perhaps even devoured all manner of books, videos, and TV specials on addiction, codependency, dysfunctional families, the child within, toxic parents, incest, or the various forms of abuse and neglect. We have attended Twelve Step meetings, ACOA meetings, Al-Anon meetings, codependency meetings, fill-in-the-blank meetings; we have attended workshops, seminars, conferences, mini-courses, support groups. Many of us have sought out the deep sorcery of Freudian analysis, Jungian analysis, strategic therapy, structural therapy, energy therapy, herbal therapy, massage therapy, crystal therapy, reprocessing therapy.

In our journey, we have learned all the acronyms, all the jargon; we have become acquainted with all the experts, all the authorities; we have become literate in all the theories, all the therapies; we have nodded to all the woes, laughed at all the inside jokes. We have, in the end, journeyed our way, earned our way, to full membership in the Righteous Society of the Eternally Victimized. Finally, we belong.

And yet, something is still missing. Yes, things are better. We are better. We no longer see ourselves as helpless inmates of our own despair and self-loathing, eternally damned by our own inadequacies and shortcomings. Yet that lush valley of normalcy we have heretofore only been able to glimpse from afar still alludes us. We have created motion around us, but we sense we have not moved the whole distance. Grief continues to well up from depths having no apparent bottom; old wounds continue to fester, occasionally to erupt into the void, only to leave behind an aftermath of regret.

We have pulled ourselves from the heart of darkness only to find ourselves again stuck, on a silty shoal perhaps, from which we can catch occasional scent of the sweet perfumes wafting from the garden that is our ultimate destination. We seem to be mired in what would surely take on the shape and texture of a quagmire—a perpetual state of woundedness, of victimhood.

What has happened to us?

What has *not* happened?

I Am a Victim

Nothing in life simply happens in isolation, without intimate and inseparable connection to a chain or web of causes and effects. Always there is at least one identifiable reason behind every event, every occurrence; most often there are several. We may not always want to acknowledge these reasons—they may not be in close harmony with the way we need, in the moment, to think about things—but they are always there. We cannot simply deny them away. And so it is in regard to all things, all aspects, about ourselves. Indeed, if we were to risk a look directly into the stark light of our truth, we would see that there are at least three identifiable, undeniable reasons why many of us become stuck in what seems, and feels, like a perpetual state of victimhood.

- **Being a victim fills our identity void.**
  One of the consequences of being victimized—of having, for example, been loved only conditionally as children—is an underdeveloped sense of self. When others were being assured they were loved just the way they were (assured not only by Mist Rogers but, far more importantly, by parents and parental s

rogates), we were being delivered a very different message: "Be who *I* need you to be, *then* I will love you." In other words, the message we internalized, and that became the master script we were to follow deep into the subsequent drama of our lives, told us that if we met the expectations (real or imagined) of others, if we pleased these others and were pleasing to them, *then* they would take us into their arms and protect us unconditionally from all the demons in all the shadows of an increasingly dark world.

This message was reinforced by cultural voices instilling in us such life-shaping notions as these two most salient ones: We can only attain the American Dream (secular happiness) if we are adequately conforming; we can only attain the Kingdom of God (spiritual happiness) if we are adequately deserving.

Consequently, many of us have spent almost the entirety of our lives—childhood, adolescence, young adulthood, even our middle-age years—trying to earn the love and acceptance that would finally open the gates to "paradise" to us. The inevitable cost has been the loss of the only personal identity and life pursuit that could have really worked for us—an authenticity that, if we were to possess it, draped over the unique configuration of our soul, would feel like a suit of clothes measured and tailored just for us.

Should we risk more than a fleeting glance over our shoulder, we would see that we have spent most of our lives being chameleons to the expectations—real, imagined, anticipated—of others. We have taken on whatever identity we thought would be pleasing to others, acted out whatever role we thought would be pleasing to these others, believed and perpetuated whatever reality we thought would be pleasing to others. We have squandered incalculable amounts of precious energy trying to fit ourselves into someone else's mold for us, and, even worse, trying to do it perfectly. We believed if we not only did it all, but did it all perfectly, the objects of our heroic efforts would have no choice: They would simply *have to* love us.

In other words, we have spent most of our lives being other than "to our own selves true." And in doing this we have had to ⁔n ever increasing level of gut-searing terror—one moment ⁔f failing to pull it off, the next moment for fear of being ⁔ as a fraud.

For us, the purple robe of victimhood is the first "store-bought" suit of clothes we've ever tried on that feels as if it were made just for us: "Ah, so *this* is who I am!" It should be of little surprise, then, that so many of us now hang on to this robe, this identity, as we perhaps once clutched the familiar form of the teddy bear who loved us in our fantasy when no one else would in our inescapable reality.

- **Being a victim gets us the attention and sympathy we never got as children.**

For many of us, our parents were too damaged and distracted by their own pain to give us the kind of attention we needed and sought as normal, needful children. Many of us interpreted this lack of attention and overt affection from our parents as a deserved punishment for something we either lacked or failed to do: Either we were inherently deficient in some way and therefore were irredeemably unlovable (a notion reinforced by our culturally ingrained concept of "original sin") or we had failed to do enough (or achieve enough) to earn their love (a notion reinforced by our culturally ingrained appease-the-angry-Father-in-Heaven paradigm).

Since learning these early lessons, we have held onto them with all the tenacity of someone, watching themselves dangle from a dizzying height in a recurrent dream, too afraid of falling to even consider letting go. For us, then, getting attention of any kind—from parents, friends, classmates, spouse, or God—has meant making ourselves worthy of it or earning it. It has never meant simply standing in place and letting it patter down on us like a warm summer shower.

Therefore, instead of spending even a single (selfish) moment singing in the rain, we have spent every waking moment becoming the best nurses, the best teachers, the best social workers, the best environmentalists, the best therapists, the best listeners on the planet. We have spent every waking moment aspiring to do the best in everything we undertook, never setting our sights on "good enough," but always on such lofty and conspicuous heights as valedictorian, Eagle Scout, star of the school play, class president, varsity letterer, above-1400 SATer, 4-minute miler, most-likely-to-succeeder, insufferable perfectionist. In trying to do, to become, to achieve all this, however, we have expended enormous amounts of energy, often to the point of complete and utter exhaustion, sometimes to the very brink of dropping into a bottomless abyss of despair.

But then, over the crest of the hill, came the cavalry! Salvation in the form of a new awareness about ourselves.

We learned of our victimhood—our particular syndrome— through a friend, or through an article in *Redbook*, or through a book recommended to us, or though *Bradshaw on the Family*, or through listening in on a conversation at our hair dresser's. However we learned about the deep pathology of our lifelong angst, our new awareness suddenly offered us a way of bringing acceptance, attention and meaning into our lives without our having any longer to jump through hoops, any longer having to contort ourselves into disingenuous molds, any longer having to wake up in the morning feeling even more tired than we did when we went to bed. We could just give ourselves over to being the victim all those new authorities and gurus in our lives said we authentically were—had an unconditional right to be. Hallelujah!

• **Being a victim excuses us from getting on with it.**
As victims, we tend to revert into the persona of that abandoned child, that wounded waif, we all harbor within. We cling to the belief, as if to life itself, that there is someone out there, a surrogate parent, who will come to our rescue, swoop us up into their strong arms and hug us against their breast until all the pain and grief, like snake venom, is squeezed right out of us, for all time. We cannot possibly rescue ourselves, for we are much too powerless, much too small, much too bruised and battered to do so. Besides, why should we have to? If anybody on this earth is deserving of being rescued, *we* are. After all, look at everything we've been through. All that hurt. All that loss. All that grief.

Likewise, we deserve justice. If not *full* restitution, *full* retribution, *full* "satisfaction," then the very least we deserve is seeing those who harmed us made painfully aware of just how much pain and loss they have caused us. Some of us may actually take it upon ourselves to seek this minimum level of justice directly, perhaps even going so far as to openly confront those who victimized us; however, most of us, having little if any history of directly confronting or challenging anyone perceived as an authority figure, will likely opt for a more indirect route.

In fact, many of us, surrendering ourselves completely to the cowering urchin within, opt for the ultimate indirect tactic and simply fantasize about getting even. Or, especially if the target of our wrath is no longer available to us (deceased, disappeared), we may generalize our need for justice by taking up a cause that allows us to identify ourselves with a kindred group (disadvantaged children, defenseless whales, disenfranchised fathers, discriminated gays, dehabitated owls) for whom and with whom we can prevail.

Whatever we do, the result will always be the same, for it cannot be otherwise: We will become more concerned with getting even than with getting on with it.

Perceiving ourselves as victim also allows us to justify pulling out the "it's not my fault" flag and waving it around for all to see. "Hey, I'm not the one who did this," we tell everybody, including (especially) ourselves, perhaps stomping our foot for emphasis. "So why should I be the one to have to repair all the damage?" In fact, once again rushing in and taking on someone else's responsibility, doing all their work for them, would be victimizing ourselves all the more. This excuse, of course, does nothing more than reinforce our child-centered need to be rescued.

Finally, there is that age-old excuse we share not only with each other but with all our "normal" idols as well: Confronted with a clear and present need to make fundamental changes (not simply rearrange the deck chairs on the Titanic), we say to ourselves: "Hey, as bad as things are now, at least I know what I'm dealing with. If I change the rules, I might end up playing a game at which I cannot succeed. This game I know. I know all the rules, I know all the moves, I know all the players. Better to feed the devil I know than to unbox the one I don't."

And so, instead of getting on with the real work, we wait at the curb to be rescued, we distract ourselves and our energies with getting even, we refuse to assume the full responsibility of repairing damage that was not our fault, and we cling to the skirts of the familiar.

• **Being a victim justifies our self-absorption.**

We live in perhaps the most self-absorbed society on earth. Few other peoples on this earth have managed to become so consummately self-preoccupied. In America, the individual reigns supreme. The Bill of Rights is the Bill of *Absolute* Rights. Our operative attitude, whether we driving down the highway or queuing up to buy tickets to the opera, is "me before thee". Our modus operandi is getting all the gusto we can get and good luck to you. If something goes wrong, it's somebody else's fault. If we make a mistake, we expect a minimum of consequences, if any at all.

If we add to this underlying self-absorption the intense kind of self-concern that comes from being in physical or emotional pain, our natural inclination is, of course, to become even more self-absorbed, perhaps even to the point of a near-total preoccupation with self. In the extreme, consider Mother Teresa holding her hand on a hot burner. How concerned in such a horrific moment would this saintly Samaritan be about the fate and welfare of the street children of Calcutta? How concerned would any of us be?

As victims, we have been traumatized by a fate not of our own making, and although we may not have our hand on a hot burner, we are in torment nonetheless. We have been wounded, betrayed, deprived, robbed, exploited, even brutalized. Who can blame us, then, if we happen to be preoccupied with self, even above what has become the cultural norm? We certainly aren't about to blame ourselves. (We're not into self-blaming anymore, thank you very much.) We have spent a good share of our lives focused on others—on others' needs and superiority. Now it's time to be focused on ourselves.

If anybody deserves a little self-preoccupation, by god, *we* do.

We are undeniably, authentically, unconditionally victims, you and I. Victims of dysfunction, neglect, exploitation, systematic violence, ritual abuse, incest, conditional love. We are ACOAs, survivors, codependents. We are a damaged and diminished child within. We are stunted trees grown from seeds cast over poisoned soil.

But is this it?

Is this all we can be? All we were meant to be?

Forest of the Essential Self

As victims, we have come to perceive ourselves as diminished, less than whole, incomplete. We feel a nagging emptiness, a gnawing hunger, that not food, not drink, not work, not achievement, not sex, not the thrill of constant crises can quite fill or satisfy. Something deep within our interior landscape is missing. Something essential.

Peering from the promontory of our new awareness, some of us have come to believe we have discovered the source of the nagging, unsettling emptiness within us: Large, sometimes desert-like gaps in the forest of our essential self. Where towering oaks of self-pride should be standing, where stately elms of self-assurance should be standing, where majestic jack pines of self-respect should be standing, where resplendent magnolias of self-love should be standing, only stunted saplings, arrested promises, are to be found—shriveled by a near life-long lack of the proper nourishment and cultivation.

Many of us are now embarked on a quest to fill these gaps in the forest of our essential self. For some of us, this has meant enlisting the aid of some form of psychotherapy, often in the form of long-term analysis, and this has been good for us: It has helped us understand what has happened to us, and it has given us permission to liberate ourselves from endless cycles of self-blame and self-flagellation—perhaps even from self-destruction. For others, this has meant swearing off diminishing addictions (everything from alcohol to potato chips)—or at least replacing them with such "enhancing" addictions as vitamin pills and aerobics. This too has been good for us, giving us a sense of self-pride and well-being, and it has taught us we can have some measure of real control over our own destiny.

But none of these measures, nor any of the other measures we may have taken to fill in the gaps in the forest of our essential self, has been enough. Despite all the hard work, all the sweat, all the sacrifice— despite all the resultant growth and foliation—something of that same old nagging emptiness lingers. However many gaps or holes in our interior landscape we may have been able to fill, there remains at least one unfilled.

Deeper within.

The Garden Within

To discover what is causing this lingering emptiness within us, we must be willing to venture well beyond the forest of our essential (secular) self. Indeed, if we are to discover the true source of our discontent, we must be willing to probe the shadows and mists of our interior landscape all the way to the very center of our being.

What is to be found there (or better, what is not to be found there) may come as something of a surprise to some, perhaps even many, of us: Despite all those fears we may secretly harbor about who and what we really are at the very core of our being (as compared to what all those good and saintly "normal" folks out there are at the very core of their being), we will not find there any drooling, fire-breathing monsters nor any slithering denizens of the Freudian id. What we will find instead is simply a fallow garden, an empty vineyard barren of all growth save for a few stunted and shriveled vines.

Just as the forest from which we have dared venture is the realm of our essential self, our ego self (see *Glossary*), the garden in which we now stand, at the very core of our being, is the realm of our spiritual self (see *Glossary*). Instead of standing fallow before our saddened eyes, like a blighted urban ghetto, this holy place should be lush with sprawling, fruiting vines, their roots reaching deeply into the Great Mystery below, their tentacles reaching upward and outward to connect us to all that is.

If we will but stand there and gaze on this dismal sight and not allow ourselves to divert our inner eyes from its terrible reality, we will at last begin to acknowledge what is perhaps the most fundamental truth of our victimhood: The most crippling damage any victim of neglect or abuse, any victim of conditional love, can suffer, whatever the particular circumstance, is not physical in nature, nor psychological; it is spiritual. It is not a broken body, nor a maimed psyche; it is a shriveled, desiccated soul.

When we allow unresolved fear and rage to accumulate in the normally crystalline skies over our inner landscape, these corrosive ethers eventually condense in the growing chill and fall as acid rain on our garden within, poisoning the very soil in which grow our essential connections to all else, to all the sources of lasting joy. As this toxic rain continues to fall over the years, the vines of our essential connections become more withered and desiccated, and we become more isolated

and alienated, more despondent and despairing. Instead of seeing ourselves as essential, contributing members of a larger whole, a community of kindred others without bounds, we become self-imprisoned in
our own private little purgatory. We become too preoccupied with our
growing agony and our deepening emptiness to give vital attention to
our garden within, to fulfill our essential role as the primary nurturers
and cultivators of our own happiness, to even recognize our role as
such.

Eventually, inevitably, like the solitary honey bee separated from the
larger community of the hive, we die in spirit.

Hope, however, does not die with us, for it cannot. Hope is the proto-
stuff from which the universe is forged. Always, there is the hope of
resurrection by our own magic.

Greening the
Garden Within

*The first peace, which is the most important, is that
which comes within the souls of men when they
realize their relationship, their oneness, with the
universe and all its Powers, and when they realize
that at the center of the universe dwells Waken Tanka,
and that this center is really everywhere,
it is within each of us.*
—Black Elk

*We must strive to allow our souls to grow in their
natural ways and to their natural depths.*
—Clarissa Pinkola Estés
Women Who Run With the Wolves

As victims, we tend to see ourselves as powerless. We are powerless in the face of our pain. We are powerless in the face of our emptiness. We are powerless in the face of our isolation. We are powerless in the face of our differentness. We are powerless in the face of our unlovableness. We are powerless in the face of our grief. We are powerless in the face of our despair. We are powerless in the face of our tragic fate. We were rendered powerless as children; we continue to be powerless as adults.

The truth is, of course, that, although we were indeed relatively powerless as children, especially in regard to the power wielded over us by our parents, we are not powerless as adults. Even a moment's open reflection will remind us that we are every bit as powerful as the most powerful success icon or authority figure we can conjure up as a basis for comparison. We are as powerful as the President of the United States, the CEO of General Motors, and the Sultan of Brunei. We are so powerful that, beginning this very moment, we can radically change the way we view our victimhood.

For example, instead of viewing our victimhood as a locked closet into which we were led blindfolded but trusting by a conspiracy of manipulating or betraying others, we can view it as a dark but familiar place that we did not originally choose for ourselves but are now choosing to remain in, unwilling to risk losing the devil we know for the one we don't. Instead of viewing it as our final destination, fated to us by forces too powerful and overwhelming to resist, we can choose to view it as a cul-de-sac we were led into by a driver who is no longer at the wheel. Instead of viewing it as the only suit of clothes that will ever feel tailor-made just for us, we can view it as a ready-made excuse for not getting on with the hard work of tailoring ourselves to fit the suit of our full potential.

We are so incredibly powerful that we can even choose to view our victimhood *not* as the cruel curse, the terrible injustice, the unforgivable wrong we perhaps need to view it as in the moment, but as the gift, the opportunity, it truly can be. Indeed, we can choose to view our victimhood as nothing less than an opportunity to ascend to a height of enlightenment, fulfillment, and spiritual development we might not otherwise have been incented, nudged, or inspired to attain. In fact, if we choose, we can assume the attitude that it is not frowning adversity that foils "success," but adversity's smiling opposite. Consider the unfortunate person born to little or no adversity—handed a silver spoon at birth. This person is not likely to ever learn how to forge practical implements out of malleable metals, to learn how to mold practical implements into artful implements, and to become a mentor to other silversmiths. This person subsequently will not know the joys of struggling, overcoming, contributing, and making a real difference.

Indeed, how we view our victimhood—as a dead end or starting point, as our destiny or an opportunity, as a curse or a gift—is entirely up to us. Power is not an issue; we have all the power and personal resources, we will ever need. What it all comes down to, simply, is making a choice—summoning the courage to do so.

The Task at Hand

The task at hand is movement—a fundamental shift away from fear and rage and toward unconditional love and compassion. We must move away from alienation and isolation, toward integration and connection; away from meaninglessness and insignificance, toward purposefulness and importance; away from despair and hopelessness, toward joy and optimism. Our task is to move our spiritual center out of the swamp of our victimhood.

We move our spiritual center when we make the kind of changes that serve to liberate us from the fierce gravity of our rage, fear, pain, and grief. We move our spiritual center when we make the kind of changes that serve to bring our alienated self into alignment with what we might view as the universal spiritual axis or core—what Black Elk called "Wakan Tanka," what the Buddha called the "immovable spot," what Jesus called "the Kingdom of God." This spiritual center of harmony and well-being is symbolized in mythologies all over the world by such metaphors as the circle (the communion wafer, Navajo sand paintings, Hindu mandala), the bowl (the chalice, the medicine pipe), the tree (the cross, the Tree of Life, the sun dance pole, the Christmas tree), the human spine (kundalini yoga), the towering mountain (Mt. Kilimanjaro, the Himalayas, the Black Hills), and the seed (the mustard seed in Jesus' parable).

In contrast, we move our secular center when we make the kind of changes that bring us little more than fleeting relief from what deeply afflicts us. We move our secular self, for example, when we move to a new job, to a new home, or to a new spouse. When we move our secular center, we change the color, shape, or texture—the presenting surface—of a problem, but we do not *solve* the problem. When we spread varnish over rotten wood, we do not fundamentally change the wood. Consider the vertical slum that replaces the horizontal slum; the "dry" drunk who replaces the "wet" drunk.

Moving our spiritual center involves asking ourselves some fundamental questions and then allowing ourselves to move in whatever direction the unfiltered, unedited answers nudge us. Please take a moment now to consider the following questions carefully:

- Do I feel a deep sense of oneness, of connectedness—a fundamental kinship with all that is, big and small, animate and inanimate, visible and invisible?

- Do I feel a deep sense of personal meaning and purpose? Do I see myself as a co-creator of something much too grand ever to be captured in words, even by the most accomplished of poets; something much too beautiful ever to be captured on canvas, even by the most sensitive of artists?

- Do I feel a deep sense of balance and harmony? Do I perceive the music in my soul as an essential part of a larger symphony?

- Do I feel a deep reverence and respect for the miracle of being, in all its kindred forms?

- Do I feel a deep sense of inner tranquillity, an absence of incessant yearning and turmoil? Do I sense a lushness, a fruitedness, in my garden within?

- Do I feel in my heart that if I were to die this day, this hour, my last thought would be no thought at all, but simply an inner smile?

If we will answer these questions with absolute candor, the amount of dissonance or turmoil they trigger will tell us precisely the degree to which the gravity of our ego self is binding us, distracting us, and holding us back from our full potential. We will find out just how far our spiritual self is being held out of alignment with the universal spiritual center, the "immovable spot," "the Kingdom of God." They will remind us of what we already know or what, in the still of an unscheduled moment, we at least have sensed: Only by moving our spiritual center can we truly get to where we need to go—can we truly get from barren to lush. As tempting as the alternative "truth" may appear, the one promoted by almost every "midway barker" in our pervasively commercialized, secularized society, moving our secular center alone—feeding only our insatiable ego self—simply will *not* do it.

Getting to Green

If we are truly to rid ourselves, once and for all, of this nagging emptiness that has been plaguing us now seemingly since birth, we must commit ourselves to doing the hard work of moving our spiritual center—of greening our garden within.

It is worth mentioning here that we are not talking about ridding our lives of all pain. As the Buddha reminds us, life is suffering. We are human, we are sentient, we are vulnerable; physical and emotional suffering cannot other than be an integral part of our lives. No matter who we are, or what our accidental circumstances, we will always know affliction, deprivation, loss, frustration, disappointment, betrayal, and a host of other little agonies. We are talking here only about ridding our lives of the kind of suffering that derives from spiritual emptiness—from the potential not yet realized, the life not yet lived.

Happiness is not the absence of pain, nor is it the experience of pleasure. Happiness is simply being able, at any point, to smile back on a life worth every moment of whatever allotment of suffering we have had to transcend.

There is, of course, no single formula, path, or process we can all universally follow in order to get to green, to lushness, any more than there is a single, "one size fits all" formula for raising a child, painting a picture, losing weight, scaling a mountain, starting a business, or writing a book. However, for any change process to be more than simply another passing fad—more a child of ego than of soul—it must embody a set of deep, authenticating principles. These principles are the raw truths that give the process its power and timelessness, just as nuggets of gold and roughs of diamond are the "raw truths" that give jewelry its untarnishable beauty. We cannot always articulate these deep truths directly, because language, always imperfect, is often inadequate to the task. However, just as we know we are in the presence of real art by the resonance it produces with deep cords within, we also know we are in the presence of real truth by the resonance it produces with even deeper cords within.

This guide book offers a strategy for greening the garden within—for moving our spiritual center—that involves building a self-directed change process around four essential tasks. These four tasks embody a set of fundamental principles that are (at least partially) reflected in the fifty-two verses of the "Daily Reminders" offered later in this book. (At this point, you may wish to pause to review these verses.) These principles are not new: They are not the Nine New Enlightenments exclusively revealed in the latest pre-millennium bestseller. Nor are they the Eleven Steps to Nirvana proffered by some newly sober celebrity attempting to jump start a flagging acting career. Instead, they are simply reminders of timeless truths of which, on some level, we are already aware and to which we have equal access. They are embodied in this book in such as way as to bring their power to bear for making fundamental changes in our equally precious, ephemeral lives.

In essence, this guide book is simply a gentle strumming across cords that lay deep within us all. It pretends to be nothing more.

Four Buzzing Bees

The approach used in this guide book for helping us move our spiritual center consists of an invitation to construct a self-directed process of change centered around four general tasks:

- Making peace with the past

- Making peace with ourselves

- Rewriting the old scripts

- Being who we really are

Although these four tasks are listed here in linear sequence and are likewise addressed in the following sections, you are encouraged to think of them as being configured in some nonlinear, non-hierarchical arrangement, perhaps in a circle or sphere; and as being dynamic rather than static, collaborating in a dance in which the energy of the one becomes the energy of the others.

For example, you might think of them as four points of light pinging around a translucent shell, their mutual motion eventually blurring into a uniform radiance of mindful energy. Or you might think of them as the blades on a ceiling fan, separate if you focus on only one, a unity if you view them as a system. Or you might think of them as four bees buzzing around the interior of a hive, their quickening dance eventually transforming their motion into a unity that fills the entire space.

The reason for taking this view is that moving our spiritual center is not a linear process: Instead of consisting of a succession of discrete, mutually exclusive tasks, it consists of our simultaneously engaging in more than one task at a time, with each task bearing some degree of influence on the others. For example, in order for us to be who we really are (our "true self"), we must behave in ways that defy the behavior we scripted for ourselves back when we needed to automate certain responses in order to survive the moment; at the same time, we must be able to let go of the grief and anger that keeps us trapped in the prison of our "false self."

First Things First

When we enter a landscape not entirely familiar to us, it is often beneficial to spend a little time looking around before we venture in any particular direction. We are less likely to make a false move, and more likely to enjoy ourselves, even if there is serious work to be done. Which there indeed is.

The following suggestions are intended to help you get oriented and comfortable:

- **Read through this guide book from cover to cover before making any judgments or taking any specific action.**

  Human beings are naturally wary of the unfamiliar. Caution and skepticism are evolved, time-proven defense mechanisms. Therefore, feel free to be as cautious as necessary about the territory covered by this guide book. Take time to explore the entire landscape before you decide whether or not to commit yourself to pitching your tent within its environs.

  You may be surprised to find that what at first appears to be unfamiliar territory is not really unfamiliar after all, even though you may never have actually visited it before. Indeed, who among us has not met someone she could not possibly have met before but whose physical presence or "aura" spawns that strange but comforting feeling of familiarity?

  Another possible benefit to pre-reading this guide book is that it will allow you time and opportunity to decide where, given who you are in the moment—the particular configuration of your unique self—you would be most comfortable entering a self-directed process of change. One size does not fit all; one process does not fit all.

When you come to the chapters in this guide that describe the four essential tasks listed earlier, you may wish to allow yourself sufficient time to fully digest each chapter before moving on to the next. You may also wish to use the meditation beginning each of these four chapters as a way of clearing your mind of "roof chatter"—the clink and clamor in your perhaps too-busy brain.

Hint: Find an oasis of quiet time to which you can consistently escape—perhaps with a mug of hot coffee—each time you commit yourself to reading a selection in this guide book. Also, resist any impulse to rush into action before you have finished reading the entire guide: Rushing into early action, however well-intentioned and earnest, might well turn out to be counter-productive in the end—as in the case of assembling a child's toy on Christmas Eve without first reading through all the instructions.

- **After completely pre-reading this guide book, enter a self-directed change process at whichever point you feel the greatest tug.**

Just as we are not all equally suited to ride a Harley-Davidson motorcycle into the sunset as a way of finding our true self (a la *Zen and the Art of Motorcycle Maintenance*), neither are we equally suited to squeeze our unique selves into the same "one size fits all" formula for moving our spiritual center. There is, in fact, no one "best" point at which to enter the paradigm for change presented in this guide book. There is only the point that feels best to each one of us. For example, for some of us *Making Peace with the Past* might feel like too much, too fast—too large an initial leap—whereas *Being Who We Really Are* might feel just right.

When we shop for new clothes, we eventually buy the blouse or the shirt that appeals to us the most. We don't sit down and analyze unto paralysis why one blouse seems to appeal to us more than another; nor do we assign relative values to each possibility in accordance with a list of "satisfaction factors" derived by an acknowledged expert in the field; nor do we allow someone other than ourselves to make the selection for us. We simply follow the gravity of our own instinct. Let this be the way you commit to doing whatever it is *you* need to do to get on with it.

• **Begin using the "Daily Reminders" at the end of this guide book as a way of stimulating introspection and maintaining focus.**

As mentioned earlier, the "Daily Reminders" offered at the end of this book are intended to reflect the deep principles on which this book is based. They are also provided as an aid for helping you maintain a focus on moving your spiritual center. You are encouraged to use this litany on a daily basis, but with the same flexibility with which you approach your overall change strategy. For example, instead of reading the entire litany in one sitting, you might wish to read and ponder only a few verses at a time. You may even wish to carry a verse or two around with you, or to stick them on certain landmarks and milestones along your daily path.

You are encouraged to supplement these "Daily Reminders" with others, from other sources. You may even wish to start composing your own. The more, the better.

One last suggestion: Translate each verse into one or more specific actions or activities that embody the essence of the message. Then carry them out, on your schedule.

• **Keep a daily journal of your thoughts and feelings.**

Keeping a journal is to self-discovery and personal change what aspirin is to a headache and grease is to a sticky wheel. Keeping a journal certainly cannot of itself "cure" us of anything, or set us free, it can indeed serve as a very powerful aid in whatever process we choose for moving our spiritual center. Among its (and therefore our) powers:

— It can help us keep ourselves focused on, and committed to, the task at hand.

— It can help us delve into depths of thought and introspection we might not otherwise attain.

— It can help us bring clarity to confusion, order to chaos.

— It can help us keep ourselves honest. (It's much more difficult to deceive ourselves with bold ink on stark paper than with phantom thoughts against a misty backdrop.)

— It can serve as a safe place for purging ourselves of perhaps a lifetime of pent-up rage.

Be forewarned, however, that keeping a journal is one of those "tasks" (like meditating) that can readily degenerate into a burden—"one more thing"—especially if we approach it with a rigid sets of expectations. Suggestion: Get a 5" x 7" notebook and commit yourself to filling only one side of one sheet of paper each day. Also, try to do your journal-writing at the same time each day, so that it becomes an integral part of your daily routine (and therefore does not involve having to make a conscious decision).

• **Scan the reading list at the end of this guide book with an eye toward beginning a reading program.**
Knowledge is power. There can be no better way of empowering ourselves, therefore—of enriching our understanding on a particular subject—than by reading about it across the widest possible spectrum of viewpoints and experiences. The reading list included with this guide book is specifically intended to help us enrich our notions about spirituality—what spirituality is (can be); what role it plays in the human experience; what role culture plays in forming our sometimes rather rigid (and therefore limited) notions about it.

The reading list provided with this guide book is not meant to be all inclusive; it is simply offered as a sampling of possible "entry points" for launching a personal reading program. You might wish to view it as just enough "seed water" to prime a pump from which you will drink as often and as much, from this day forward, as your thirst for true empowerment requires.

• **If your modus operandi involves laying down formal plans and schedules, keep these as flexible as you possibly can.**
Many of us tend to operate in a way that makes us feel in control (control is safety) and that does not allow much room for

flexibility (flexibility is danger of losing control). For example, we make very specific plans and then tend to view these plans as the Ten Commandments, and we make very specific (unrealistic!) schedules and then tend to regard these schedules as chiseled in granite. Needless to say, in a world in which it is almost never possible to predict more than a few of the variables that might impact on any plans we might lay down, much less actually control them, this modus operandi often ends up causing us more problems than it solves.

You may wish to keep in mind, therefore, that our object here is simply to set something—a process—into motion, not to completely preordain the path that this process ultimately takes, not to control it to the point that it can only suffer from such control, not to decide ahead of time just exactly the way everything must go, and not to play God to a universe of our own making.

Suggestion: Let your "gut"—your inner voice—be your guide. If this voice, speaking in visceral pulses of deep logic rather than in rushing streams of words, tells you to start at point C, rather than at point A, then start at point C; if it tells you to proceed with caution, then proceed with caution; if it tells you to take a walk and think about it, then take a walk and think about it. (While you're walking, keep at least one eye looking outward. Who knows what serendipitous something you might encounter?)

- **Refer back to this guide book often during the early stages of your change process.**

No matter where you choose to begin your change process, the route you ultimately take will not be linear. That is, it will not be a typical progression from step 1 to step 2, from step 2 to step 3, and so forth. Instead, you will find that everything you do simultaneously affects everything else, directly or indirectly. Indeed, your movement will be more of an expansion (growing into a larger self) than a progression (moving to a "higher" plane).

For this reason, you will likely need to return frequently to this guide book, especially at the beginning stages of your self-directed process. Not only will doing this help facilitate your being pulled in the direction best for you in the moment, it will also help you to become engaged in the suggested exercises .

Mixing Our Metaphors

Many of us were told in school never to mix our metaphors. It was offensive to some deep principle, we were made to believe, one likely never satisfactorily articulated. Should we be scolded, then, for using both "greening your garden within" and "moving your spiritual center" to capture essentially the same concept? If we consider only the rule we grew up with, then the answer cannot be other than "Yes." But if we consider the full context of what we are attempting to accomplish in this book, then the answer might be in the contrary.

The true test of "correctness"—whether in regard to English usage or personal conduct—is never whether we adhere strictly to an arbitrary rule that purports to hold a universal truth, but whether we have sufficiently addressed the unique needs of a particular situation. Rules can guide us; only context can tell us what is the *right* thing to do in a particular moment. If the light is red and you are tired and impatient, the right thing to do is to sit and wait. If the light is red and you are on the way to the hospital because your five-month-old infant has stopped breathing, the right thing to do is to lay on the horn and *go*. Context is everything.

What this "everything" is in any particular context is always available to us, for the simple reason that every context, even one of near or complete emptiness, has its own voice—felt or sensed rather than heard. The voice emanating from the whirlwind of our chronic angst, our chronic unhappiness, is an example. If we were to still our inner-selves sufficiently to hear it—*feel* it—this voice would likely tell us that the source of our perennial discomfort is a gnawing hunger for vital *spiritual* essences.

Further, it would likely tell us that we are essentially deaf to this need because we lack sufficient language with which to probe beyond the limited notions on human spirituality we have acquired from traditional influences. So limited are these notions, in fact, that if we were to be so daring as to audibly utter the word "spirituality" at a cocktail party, we would likely suffer the same fate as we would were we to roll up our sleeves to reveal an armful of oozing body sores.

This is unfortunate, but it is the reality and context in which most of us have been forged and molded. This context tells us that if we are to enrich our notions about spirituality we must first enrich the language with which we attempt to communicate and examine these notions.

Before we journey any further into the perhaps-unfamiliar landscape of this guide book, therefore, let us dare to use a third metaphor, or model, to help us enhance our notions about this elusive essence we call "spirituality." Under this third model, our spirituality consists of a luminous aura that extends outward from an undiminishable spark that lies at the very center of our being. The luminosity of this aura depends on the degree to which we unconditionally extend acceptance and compassion to others, to which we unconditionally give of self. It is at once a measure of our connection (oneness) with all else and a measure of our true happiness (bliss), for the one is the other.

At one extreme, the gravity of the accumulated mass of our ego self is so strong that no illumination is able to radiate outward from our spiritual center; our ego self is essentially a black hole, completely and wholly focused on itself. We are the most miserable of human souls. At the other extreme, our ego self is essentially transparent, massless, and the spark of goodness that dwells within us glows like a single candle standing in an unshuttered window, its soft radiance seeming to fill the darkness inside and out. We are the happiest, most blissful, of souls. (Somewhere between these two extremes, hopefully biased more toward the latter, lies the best we can hope to achieve as mortal beings.)

In other words, to the degree we allow our *body mind* (see *Glossary*) to become focused on the needs (real or imagined) of our secular self— to the degree that we perceive our secular self to be threatened or vulnerable—we tend to shrink or limit our context of inclusion and concerns. At the extreme, we pull ourselves into a fetal ball of utter self-absorption; we become an infant whose insatiable, innumerable needs fill the full volume of its universe of concern.

This limited context of concern and inclusion, in turn, tends to limit our notions about who we are ("we must be the person they want us to be"), what will bring us true happiness ("absence of pain"), what our purpose in life is ("get through another day"), and what our relationship to others should be ("get them to like me"). As we are able to diminish the demands of our ego self, however, we find ourselves naturally embracing an ever larger context of concern and inclusion, thereby enriching our notions about who we are ("the unique self we were meant to be"), what will bring us true happiness ("giving of self"), what our purpose in life is ("using our gifts to make a difference"), and what our relationship to all else should be ("to acknowledge the common miracle at the sacred core of all being").

We could mix our metaphors even further, because spirituality is a richness of being that requires of us a richness of color and texture if we are to adequately capture it on the canvas of our understanding. However, there comes a time.

There Comes a Time

No matter how awkwardly we mix our metaphors or how miserably we fail to capture in words or images that which, in truth, can never be transmuted into the intimately familiar, the deep truth remains: As human beings, we can only be as fulfilled as we are able to extend the embrace of our unconditional giving to others, to extend the embrace of our inclusion and acceptance of others, to extend the embrace of our compassion and concern for others. To the extent we limit this embrace, and therefore the context of our notions about what life is all about (who we are as unique individuals, what will bring us true happiness, what our purpose is, and what our relationship to all else needs to be), we condemn ourselves to a state of spiritual purgatory, we tether ourselves teasingly, tormentingly just short of paradise's eternally wide-open door.

Indeed, there comes a time to stop talking about what it is we need to do, where it is we need to go, and to simply get on with the business of doing it. There comes a time for us to say out loud, for benefit of our own ears, "If a single picture of what might be is indeed worth a thousand words about what might be, then a single act toward what might be is worth a thousand pictures of what might be."

This guide book is not another passive "feel good" salve for aching souls, contrived to reassure and lull by telling us the three messages we most like to hear: it won't hurt; it won't make me sweat; it won't take me more than five minutes a day. This guide book is instead a call to action, an invocation to get on with it, an offering of at least one way we, as victims, can comfortably (at our own pace, along our own path) go about greening our garden within, aligning our spiritual center, illuminating our aura of connection and fulfillment. It is a guiding hand that can, if we will but reach out and meet it half way, gently lead us toward:

- Making peace with a past of betrayal and woundedness

- Making peace with the part of us who has injured others

- Rewriting the old scripts that no longer serve our, or anybody else's, best interests

- Acknowledging and becoming the authentic, one-of-a-kind person we were meant to be

There comes a time . . . .

Guiding Hand

An open hand is being extended toward you. It is a broad hand of obvious strength, with thick, muscular fingers, but you are not afraid. You know this to be a gentle hand, for only weakness, you have learned, seeks to do harm for its own sake. Reaching out, you grasp this open hand firmly, feeling it grasp yours in equal measure. Giving yourself over to a firm, but gentle tug, you allow yourself to be led where you need to go.

You are standing atop a gentle knoll, overlooking a vast wind-swept meadow of billowing daisies and black-eyed Susans—of white and gold. The steady breeze is like a gentle flow of tepid water bathing over your face. You can hear it eddying playfully in your ears. Through your nose, you draw in a slow, deep breath of the sweet-scented air, hold it a moment, then let it out. You draw in another breath, hold it a moment, let it out. You then lift your face until it is fully immersed in the warm, healing rays of the sun. Your whole being begins to glow with the life-giving radiance of this timeless miracle. It is you and you are it.

From overhead, you hear the stirring call of a solitary eagle. Shading your eyes with one hand, you watch this magnificent creature circle majestically against a backdrop of bottomless blue, seemingly without effort, as if riding the buoyancy of a wisdom only it can discern. Suddenly, with perfect grace, it swoops downward in a fluid arc and alights on your shoulder. The razor-sharp talons are firm on your tender flesh, but they do not pierce it. Looking into the bottomless eye looking into yours, you sense you are in the presence of the sacred.

Watching the eagle wing its way back skyward, you feel the empty wake of its absence, but you do not feel abandoned. There is a bond between you now, one that can never be diminished by distance, however great.

It is you and you are it.

You are feeling weary now, so you scan for a place to rest. For a moment you feel the sun-shrouding shadow of an old guilt, but then you remember: It is always OK to rest when you are weary—always. You see an ancient oak holding beneficent dominion over the billowing fields, so you float through the sea of white and gold and take safe harbor in the mottled shade provided by the old oak's out-

spreading branches. Although the massive trunk is unyielding to the back of your heavily fatigued head, you find a spot that is concave in just the right places to fit the bumps uniquely your own; there is always such a spot for us, if only we will look for it.

The ground beneath you is blanketed with a lush quilt of mint-green moss. Comfortable now, you close your eyes, feeling the soft warm breeze on the outside gradually become a soft warm breeze on the inside—sweeping through the endless meadow of white and gold that lies deep within you.

It is you and you are it.

You draw in a deep breath of the sweet-scented miracle of you, hold it a moment, then let it out. You draw in another deep breath, hold it a moment, let it out. You then listen to the cacophonous clownings of a mockingbird perched in a branch high above you. How ridiculous this bird is, you murmur to yourself—this creature perched up there mimicking the calls and scolds of a dozen other birds, for no reason other than the pure joy of it. How ridiculous indeed—doing something just for the pure joy of it.

It is you and you are it.

It is time to return now, so you grasp the hand again extended toward you, and allow its gentle strength to help you up to your feet. For a moment you feel the sun-shrouding shadow of an old guilt, but then you remember: It is always OK to accept a little help from a kindred other—always.

When you open your eyes, you will find yourself standing in your garden within, tools in hand, poised over the humus of your soul.

The place you need to be.

Making Peace
with the Past

*When very bad things happen to people, they develop
a special quality of compassion that raises them to a
higher level of being.*
—Cloé Madanes
Sex, Love, and Violence

*What I have discovered is the healing power of
forgiveness. With that gift, I now can get on with my life.*
—Eric Lomax
(A British prisoner of war in World War II [one of the builders of
the bridge over the River Kwai], upon finally forgiving the Japanese
who brutally tortured him)

Comprendre c'est pardonner. (To understand is to forgive.)
—Germaine de Staöl

No one stuck in the past is going to venture very far into the future
of his or her unique potential. We all know this—we all have access to
the same bicameral magic. Yet how many of us act accordingly? The
bus keeps stopping at the curb, opening the door to us, but there we
continue to sit, as if bubble-gummed to the bench, sweltering in the
suffocating humidity of our discontent.

As victims, we become trapped in the past when we allow ourselves
to be controlled by the Mister Hyde of our unresolved pain and anger,

rather than by the Doctor Jekyll of our unconditional love and compassion. We become trapped when we allow ourselves to become preoccupied with the terrible harm that was done to us, on the perpetrators of this harm. In order to liberate ourselves, therefore, we have no other choice than to purge the larder of our soul of all that pain and anger that our "good" Mister Hyde is greedily gorging himself on.

There simply is no other way.

For many of us, actually accomplishing this—purging ourselves of all that festering pain and anger may seem like one of the most difficult things we could ever be asked to do, because it unavoidably involves making peace with those who have failed us, those who have betrayed us, those who have stolen from us. In truth, however, it is actually one of the easiest things we can ever be called on to do, because it requires no more of us in the moment than we simply choose to begin a process that might lead us to where we, until now, may have believed only "normal," "better" people could ever go.

Indeed, in this era of disempowerment and helplessness, making peace with the past requires no more of us than that we exercise the one power we all hold that no force on this earth can ever diminish or take away from us, in whole or in part: the power to make a choice, to commit ourselves to a goal, and to steer our spiritual center in a self-selected direction. We can be denied equal access to the penthouse suite by invisible glass ceilings; we can be stripped of our dignity and our humanity by exploitive, emotionally constipated bottom-line managers; we can be bound in snarls of red tape by legions of Lilliputian bureaucrats; we can be disenfranchised of our suffrage by moneyed oligarchies of self-interest; we can be denied equal access to education and neighborhoods by emperors wearing no clothes. However, we can never be denied our power to choose hope over despair, making peace with the past over hanging self-destructively onto it.

Hope—making peace with the past—moves us forward; despair—hanging onto the past—holds us back: Hope lightens our load, hanging on adds to it. What's more, while the hope we choose for ourselves moves us forward, the very act of our moving forward generates hope, which in turn moves us forward—much as the forward motion of a car drives the alternator that in turn produces the spark that keeps the car moving forward. Likewise, while the despair we choose holds us back, the very act of our being held back, of dwelling in the past, generates despair, which in turn holds us back.

What we have, then, are two recursive, self-perpetuating cycles, or spirals: A downward spiral of hopelessness and despair, and an upward spiral of hopefulness and bliss—the one leading to rage and victimhood, the other to compassion and liberation. The choice at hand for us all, then, unavoidably, is whether to move our spiritual center or keep it safely and comfortably right where it is.

If we choose to make the leap, the following steps will take us to where we need to go:

- Build a context of understanding

- Forgive those who have harmed us

Before making any decisions about these steps and their overall purpose, you may wish to read this entire chapter, as well as the following chapters . This strategy will allow you to build a context on which to base a realistic decision in regard to whether "making peace with the past" is the optimal point for you to enter a self-directed change process. Context is everything.

Building a Context of Understanding

When our circle of concern collapses to the sound of water dripping from a leaky faucet (the one we have been putting off fixing for the past six or seven months) the incessant pulses soon amplify into a relentless pounding, and our ability to give ourselves over to sleep is all but lost. The same is true when our circle of understanding encompasses no more than the failures and betrayals of those who have harmed us in some way. The incessant ache of these failures and betrayals amplifies until they take on the magnitude of deliberate acts of evil, and our ability to give ourselves over to compassion becomes all but lost.

Indeed, it is easy, and probably unavoidable, for us to "evilize" any act we view out of context. For example, when we hear on the car radio that some father, about to be divorced by his wife, has murdered both his wife and their two preschool children, we immediately judge this man a monster, deserving not one whit of our compassion. There is no context here, other than the unspeakable acts and the faceless perpetrator of these acts, and whenever there is no context, there can be no sense of proportion or perspective; everything becomes independent and absolute: The "evil" father is unconnected to anything other than his "evil" acts.

However, nothing in this world—no act, no object, no person—is independent and absolute; nothing is entirely of its own design; nothing steers a course entirely of its own choosing. Everything occurs within a context of mutual influence; everything is "in relation to." The earth pulls on the moon and creates the lunar calendar; the moon pulls on the earth and creates the tides. The sun pulls on the earth and creates the seasons; the earth pulls on the sun's radiations and creates the aurora borealis. Everything is influenced by the context of which it is an integral part; everything exerts influence on the context of which it is an integral part.

Consider yourself. To what extent are you, at this very moment, captain of your own ship? How much of who you are, what you are, even where you are—geographically, socially, philosophically, economically, psychologically, even spiritually is of your own conscious choosing, independent of all else, all others? Is, for example, your native intelligence of your own choosing? Your body type (build)? Is where on this planet you live and work entirely of your own choosing? Was the subject matter and means by which you were educated of your own choosing? Is everything you presently believe about yourself and others, as well as about the nature of your world, entirely of your own conscious choosing? Was the nurturing environment in which you were brought up of your own choosing? Is everything you currently value and aspire to entirely of your own choosing? Is how you behave toward others—your spouse, your children -entirely of your own choosing?

Or, indeed, are all of these things about you, either in whole or in part, the result of the confluence of perhaps a host of influences, visible and invisible, near and far, recognized and unrecognized?

No one enters this world all-powerful and wholly enlightened. In fact, quite the opposite is true: We come into this world wholly dependent on others, virtually powerless, and void of all understanding except what little has been intertwined into our DNA as raw instinct (e.g., empty stomach means wail like hell; pressure below means open up the flood gates). From that first moment on, driven by our deepest calling, we seek the independence and enlightenment we could not be gifted with at birth but which we must all possess, first to ensure mere physical survival, then to attain some measure of liberating comfort and leisure, finally to strive toward ultimate fulfillment. In other words, we seek out and gradually acquire the means of transforming ourselves from essentially ego-trapped, self-centered beings into liberated, unconditionally compassionate beings. How far any of us gets along this common journey toward ultimate fulfillment depends not on ourselves alone (on our initial "gifts') but on the interplay of ourselves and a myriad of other factors and influences.

None of us can sort out all the variables that contribute to what we call "fate," any more than, given a can of custom-mixed paint, we can identify all the constituent colors, much less their precise proportions. Nor can any of us say precisely where "fate" leaves off and "free will," in the form of personal responsibility and control, begins; philosophers have been asking and attempting to answer these questions for as long as our race has been able to form questions. All we can know with any certainty is:

None of us exists in isolation.

None of us is what we are entirely of our own choosing.

There are reasons for everything, including reasons for our being, at any particular point, who and what we are.

That our failures, as well as our successes, are always a product of a host of factors far too numerous and intertwined ever to be sorted out and assigned relative "blame."

None of us is born angry.

None of us is born self-loathing.

None of us is born humiliated or shamed (see *Glossary*).

None of us is born "bad."

None of us is born "evil."

Some of us may indeed become these things, just as the balsam fir "born" near the tree line becomes gnarled and stunted instead of straight and tall. However, if we can somehow take a sufficient number of steps backward from the compelling myopia of our immediate pain and anger, we can readily see that there were reasons and circumstances that shaped people into who they have become and drew them into doing what they have done; there was a context of influence and legacy, unique from ours, unique from all others. Indeed, who among those who manage to escape the disfiguring extremes of "fate" can say with any certainty that, given the same mix of circumstances handed to another vulnerable, inherently imperfect human being, they would not have ended up being and doing the same as this unfortunate "cousin"? *"There but for the grace of God. . . ."*

Had we been given an opportunity to build a context around the father who murdered his wife and two children, for instance, we would have discovered that this 26-year-old man had recently been "abandoned" by an employer as part of a "strategic downsizing," had previously been laid off by several other employers for similar reasons, had been abandoned by a total of thirteen foster families (before rescuing himself from this vicious cycle by getting himself arrested and put in jail), had been abandoned by a drug-addicted mother/prostitute when he was two-and-a-half, had been abandoned by a father he had never known. He had been physically abused by three of his fee-for-service foster parents, one of whom had burned his genitals with cigarettes for "misbehaving" (taking too much food from the refrigerator).

What this all comes down to, once again, is something we all know in our hearts, whether or not we are ready in the moment to give ourselves over to the unavoidable truth of it: Liberation from the hell-fire of our own pain and rage can only come to us through our own compassion; we can extend our compassion no further than the limits of our understanding. In other words, we ultimately can be truly our own person, be truly powerful, be truly free, be truly at peace, only to the extent we can build a context of understanding and enlightenment.

Once again, context is everything.

Coming to understand this, though, is the easy part. The hard part is actually building a context of understanding around someone from our past who has become a lingering source of pain or anger for us, thereby distracting us from getting on with what our lives are really supposed to be all about. There are, however, at least two readily available means by which we can at least begin to build a context of understanding around any person who has caused us harm, however grievous this harm may have been. Both of these context builders involve actively introducing new information into whatever context currently exists.

The first context builder, which we will arbitrarily label discovering, introduces information that is specific to a particular situation or person. The second, which we will label enriching, involves introducing general information about such powerfully molding contextual forces as culture, values, religion, and gender.

Discovering

One way to build a context of understanding is to discover specific information about people in our past who have done us great and lingering harm. However, before we pursue this course of context-building in detail, let us pause a moment to assure ourselves about the exact scope of our intentions: Our only objective here is to free ourselves sufficiently of pain and anger, of our hold on the past, such that we can at least begin to be compassionate toward those who, when we view them as we might view insects under a microscope, may appear to be monsters undeserving of any kind of moral sympathy from us or from anyone else. Our intention is to let go. It is not to let anybody off the hook; it is not to excuse anyone from being fully accountable for their actions—past, present, or future.

Though it may at first seem like a paradox, there is no conflict between being compassionate toward someone and holding this person fully accountable for their actions. For example, if someone has abused you physically or sexually, and there is reason to believe this person has harmed or is currently harming others, you can be compassionate toward this person (unvengeful) and at the same time choose to notify civil authorities about the danger this person may pose to the public. In fact, there would be little compassion involved in knowingly, or even suspectingly, allowing a perpetrator to run free to harm others (and therefore, inevitably, him- or herself).

Our Goal. Our immediate goal is modest. It is not to assemble a complete biography about someone we may feel we already know everything we'll ever want to, thank you very much. Rather, it is simply to bring into the current picture we have of this person a few bits of additional information, just enough to serve as a sort of catalyst or triggering event to crystallize out of the void a larger reality, one that, for reasons wholly understandable, we have not previously been able to bring to bear to provide a sense of proportion and perspective to some very powerful perceptions we have about our past. Our goal, then, is to enrich our context of understanding to the point we can begin to view someone disproportionately large in our life as a flawed human being rather than as a fallen angel.

In the cartoon world, when an artist wishes us to perceive a surface—a wall or chimney, for example—as a matrix of innumerable stones or bricks, she does not spend hour upon hour drawing in each and every stone or brick, because she knows she does not need to. She only needs to include a few stones or bricks in the picture—one here, one there—just enough to suggest the full reality to our willingly complicit minds. In the world of physics, water in a glass can be super cooled below thirty-two degrees Fahrenheit, such that we only need to ping the edge of the glass with our finger, as a triggering event, for the liquid to crystallize into a solid cylinder of ice. Our job, then, is to find a few stones or bricks of information we can use to suggest a full matrix of understanding; it is to reach out and ping the edge of the glass of super-cooled understanding with our finger.

In any context in which we must exercise our judgment, we need to assemble as much pertinent information as we possibly can, because each bit of information adds to the cumulative value of all the other bits. For example, if we had intentions to invest in the stock market, we would want to assemble all the pertinent information about individual companies or mutual funds and the overall economic climate that we possibly could. We would read newspapers, business journals, investment guides, and we would ask a lot of questions of many different sources. In other contexts, however, we need only to assemble a few bits of information, because each bit, rather than adding cumulatively to the whole, actually represents the whole.

For example, let's say we have spent most of two or three decades focused on our parents' failures toward us, on all the agony and torment that these failures cumulatively caused us. We raged, wept, and sank deeper into a seemingly bottomless pit of despair. Perhaps we even considered taking our own life, or we at least toyed with the idea, as a cat sometimes toys with the fate of a dazed mouse. Finally, perhaps more by chance than by design, we were able to glean just enough information from our mother to allow us to view her in an entirely different light: That is, as a forgivably flawed human being, rather than as an unforgivably flawed fallen angel. What few bits of information she shared with us would barely constitute a footnote in the larger context of her life story. Yet it was the whole story—the whole stone wall, the whole brick chimney. It was the ping against the rim of a glass filled with super-cooled liquid. Perhaps she simply told us about a single time in her own childhood in which she felt betrayed or agonizingly diminished.

Suddenly, our mother was no longer the fallen angel she had appeared when we had viewed her out of the full context of her own pain. She was simply another player, another flawed human being in a larger tragedy that we both shared, as equals, as peers, as fellow travelers. She was us, and we were her. Whereas, until this moment we had been narrowly focused on ourselves, drawn inward by our own pain, seeing not through the eyes of our adult-self but through those of our wounded-child self, the one still waiting for her parents to rescue her, to love her unconditionally, to peer magically into her soul and respond to her every need, her every hurt. Now we could see our parents almost as if *we* had become the parent, they the child.

We were free, and they were free. We were free to let go of perceptions that were really self-imprisoning chains wrought of rage, grief, hopelessness, and despair. Our parents were free to be who they could never otherwise be.

The Process. There is, of course (thank goodness!), more than one way to acquire such powerfully freeing bits of information about our parents (or about others), spanning a range from the very direct to the very indirect. If your parents are no longer living, or are otherwise unavailable to you, you are obviously limited to more indirect ways.

Here are approaches for you to consider. If for no other purpose, you may use these suggestions to stimulate your own imagination:

- **Come right out and ask.**

   The most obvious approach to acquiring key information about our parents' lives is to come right out and ask them. However, this approach is not for everybody. Indeed, if some sage authority figure were to suggest to you that this approach was it, the only way, you'd probably feel an immediate impulse to either turn and run or to do this person grievous physical harm. For many of us, the "Say, dad, how was it for you when you were a kid?" approach is just not possible for a phone call after 5:00 p.m. from the office. Forget it.

   Actually, though, by employing just a modicum of guile (let's call it "creativity"), the direct approach may not be as difficult as you might think. For example, if you wish to gain at least an inkling of how your father was treated (really treated) by his own father, you might initiate a conversation with him by issuing a one-down statement (one that appears to put him in a position of control or greater power), followed by a non-threatening query that sets the stage for even further probings.

For example, you might start off a conversation with your father by saying something like: "Say, Dad, could you give me a little advice, please? I'm in a real quandary over how I should be disciplining the kids. Spanking seems to be a real no-no these days. It's gotten so, if the neighbors hear you doing it, they call the cops. What do you think I should do?" If your father spanked (or worse) you as a child, he may respond to your request largely by justifying his own behavior. If he does, avoid challenging him or otherwise allowing yourself to be drawn into anything resembling an argument; just let him say whatever he feels he has to say within the context you have placed him. Then, at the right moment, you might follow up with something like: "Did your father spank you when you were a kid?" Your father's response to this little sleight of hand may amount to little more than the usual avoidance and denial. Then again, you might get a greater outpouring of the truth than you ever thought possible. This approach is probably worth a try. Maybe even more than one.

Of course, there are infinite variations on this theme, and only you know which ones, if any, might work in your particular situation (context is everything). You may be pleasantly surprised with the results you end up getting over time, especially if you are patient. You may even be surprised to discover that your parents have been waiting, perhaps for most of their own troubled lives, for just such an opportunity to "let it all out"—waiting for someone simply to ask.

- **Ask a relative or close family friend.**

Indirect questioning can take many forms and can be either a necessity or a choice. If your parents are no longer living, the indirect approach is unavoidably a necessity. If they are still living, it *may* be necessity, especially if your relationship with your parents is such that a direct approach could not possibly be successful, no matter how much energy you might resolve to put into it.

One indirect approach is to query a relative or a close family friend—anyone who knew your parents when they were young or who may have intimate knowledge about your parents' experiences as children. Your grandparents, if still living, are obvious candidates, but they may not be the best sources, for obvious reasons. Uncles and aunts are also possible candidates. Other possibilities could be the best man or maid of honor in your parents' wedding, a high school or college classmate with whom they are still in correspondence (check their Christmas card list for addresses), a drinking buddy, or the person your parent calls whenever he or she needs to talk to somebody.

Once you have selected a candidate, you may wish to approach this person by asking him or her for help with a family genealogy you are researching for posterity, or with a biography you are putting together as part of an upcoming family event (a milestone birthday, for example). If you include your resource conspicuously in your project—as a key figure in your genealogy or biography, for example—there is no end to the kind of information you may get simply for the asking.

• **Trade places.**

Another indirect approach is to "become" your parents as children: to enter their childhood by "walking in their moccasins." Left to our own devices, most of us likely would never think of this approach, much less actively consider it, because we have a strong tendency, even as "mature" adults, to view our parents as being very different from us, as being of vastly different proportions, as existing on an entirely different plane. Trading places with them would constitute too unthinkable a notion even to bring to conscious light.

This taboo against placing ourselves on the same plane with our parents is probably a carryover both from the way we regarded our parents when were we very young, and likely even more lacking than we are now in a sense of intrinsic worth, and from the way they regarded us, and likely still regard us, well into our adulthood: as less than complete, less than competent, less than worthy...'less than."

Interestingly, the more we view our parents as being different from us, the more we hold them to higher standards, the more difficult it is for us to be compassionate toward them.

Even though the chasm (real or imagined) that separates us from our parents may be a real Grand Canyon, there is no chasm that cannot be at least narrowed through the mere act of trading places with them, of projecting ourselves into their experience, even if only for a few moments—especially when they were, say, about five or six years old.

Though there is certainly more than one way of accomplishing this, perhaps one of the more practical ways is as follows: Visit the home, neighborhood, and, if possible, the school where you lived when you were about five or six years old. Do this mentally if you are not able to do it in person; opt for the physical presence, though, if you possibly can.

Once you have reimmersed yourself in this familiar environment, allow yourself to relive old memories freely, no matter how painful these memories might be. Allow yourself to feel them, to reexperience them, as opposed to simply viewing them in selective retrospect, from a safe distance, as you might photographs in an old family album. Let all the loneliness, abandonment, fear, betrayal, self-blame, and rage—the whole kaleidoscope of agonies, big and small, that formed you—gush to the surface.

Now visit the home, neighborhood, and, if possible, the school where your father or mother grew up. If possible, take along an old photo of your parent when he or she was under ten years old. Immersed in your parent's past, as best you can, recall the feelings you experienced when you recently reimmersed yourself in your own past. Ask yourself if what you experienced as a child was likely any different from what your parent experienced.

Ask yourself if the person who injured or betrayed you was a demon who intentionally abused his or her power over you, or if this person was simply another link in a forged chain of damaged, flawed human beings, reaching back God knows how far over the horizon of your understanding. Did this person deliberately pass on to you a very real but largely invisible legacy of accumulated agony, or did she do this because she was never able to achieve, through no real fault of her own, the level of awareness you have now managed to achieve?

Please keep in mind that our intention here is not to let anybody off the hook of personal responsibility. It is simply to bring ourselves to a point of understanding such that we can let go of the pain and anger that is holding us back. We know that, as long as we keep our focus narrow and exclusionary, we will remain stuck, just as we will remain sleepless as long as we concentrate on the thundering sound of the water dripping in the bathroom sink.

• **Defend your parent in court.**

Any suggestion that we actually "defend" the very person who damaged us may seem more like an attempt to inflict further pain on us than as a beneficent means of getting past our current pain. But, as we shall see, it is indeed the latter. Actually, this approach is simply an amalgamation of the previous two approaches, involving both discovery and empathy.

In this approach, you visualize yourself serving as your parent's defense attorney, arguing his or her case before a jury that will collectively determine whether your parent is to be paid back in kind ("eye for an eye") or shown compassion. What kind of information would you gather and present to this jury? Where would you get this information: What questions would you ask and of whom would you ask them? Why would this information be important for the jury to know? What would you be striving to accomplish with this information? In what context would you ask the jury to place your parent as they pass judgment on him or her?

Now switch places: You are the one being judged, for all the injuries or shortcomings you have inflicted on your own family, and one of your own children (or your spouse) is your advocate.

Enriching

Another way we can help ourselves build a liberating context of understanding is to enrich, or supplement, the specific knowledge we discover about specific individuals with general knowledge that pertains to all individuals. In fact, it is probably true that the more we enrich our context of understanding with general knowledge about human nature, the fewer bits of specific knowledge we require in order to reach a given level of enlightenment.

One way to appreciate the power of this kind of knowledge is to view it as the background that gives definition to whatever stands in the foreground, in the way that the shadows in an Ansel Adam's photograph give definition to the objects in the foreground. The deeper the shadows in the background, the sharper the definition of the truths in the foreground.

What we are actually doing when we enrich our context of understanding is, of course, building an intuition. In the present case, we are building an intuition about human nature, about the human soul. If we view ourselves as a science-oriented "brain," and we aspire to become a Nobel Laureate, we would likely spend a great deal of our time and energy building an intuition about one of the sciences, just as Einstein did in physics. If we view ourselves as a professional coach, and we aspire to achieve Hall of Fame repute, we would likely spend a great deal of our time and energy building an intuition about a major sport, just as Vincent Lombardi did in football. If we view ourselves as a national leader, and we aspire to become a figure of historical proportions, we would likely spend the lion's share of our time and energy building an intuition about politics and statesmanship, just as Harry Truman did.

The possibilities are legion and, as in the case of the above examples, mostly motivated by and for the needs of our ego self. However, this is often at the expense of perhaps the most important intuition any of us can build for ourselves, which is an intuition about who we are as sentient beings: what human beings really need; what forces, insidious and overt, shape us; how we react to spiritual pain.

We live in a culture that greatly emphasizes the secular over the spiritual, building a practical (vocational) intuition over building a spiritual one. We can see this emphasis in especially high relief when we compare "higher" education of today against what such an education was originally intended to be and actually did become in a few, brief contexts. Indeed, once upon a time, the central intent of a higher education was to liberate us from what would otherwise be almost certain servitude to our body mind: to build and enrich our context of understanding and enlightenment so that every choice would have a spiritual, or moral, dimension to it. Hence, it became known as a "liberal" education. Today, even though we still use the same term, the liberal education has been all but subverted into a smorgasbord of "pre-professional" and "vocational" programs that have little to do with building an intuition about human nature and human spirituality, but a great deal to do with building a portfolio of "marketable skills" and "knowledge assets." Body mind has not only prevailed over spirit mind (see *Glossary*, under *body mind*), it has all but crushed it.

However, there is still much we can do to fill the void, especially in regard to building a capacity for universal understanding and universal compassion. No matter what our particular circumstances might be, we all have at our disposal at least two powerful means, or tools, for achieving exactly this end: reading and observing.

These two tools are meant to be used as complements, each augmenting or extending the work of the other, like a pick and shovel. However, your personal "style" may be such that you feel naturally inclined to favor one over the other, perhaps even almost to the exclusion of the other. If this is true for you, then simply "go with the flow." In no way does a personal style or preference for using these two tools (or anything else) make you deficient or lacking. It means nothing more than that this is one more way we exhibit difference, that nature implements her diversity strategy. At the same time, however, you may wish to view yourself as a dynamic being who is always in process, always experimenting, always full of surprises (even to yourself).

• Reading

When someone exhorts us to read, we tend to respond in one of two ways: "Oh goody!" or "Oh gawd." Either we'd find more joy snuggling up to a good book (with a cat on our lap, a mug of hot tea or coffee at our side) than in winning the State Lottery, or we'd rather sit and watch the worst of all possible sitcoms on "the tube" than crack open the book we got from Aunt Jane last Christmas (and hate ourselves all the way to the refrigerator between programs). If we fall into the first group, the task at hand is an easy, even joyous, one: Simply grab our book bag and head for the library, taking the list of questions suggested below with us, to use as a reading guide. If we fall into the second category, however, we may at this point be somewhat inclined to skip to the next section.

Magical in its power and egalitarianism, reading enables us, without exception, to travel as widely and deeply into the human experience as we choose to venture. It allows us, without exception, to discover as much truth about the nature of our common being as we can possibly grasp. Reading liberates us, empowers us—truly informs us. Indeed, the more we learn about the complexities and intricacies of human nature, the more likely we are to understand and appreciate the ways in which things can and do go wrong in human beings, the terrible degree to which things can and do go wrong, and, perhaps most importantly, why they go wrong and why sometimes they stay wrong, generation after generation.

The scope of inquiry being alluded to is much too rich and broad to attempt to make it "manageable" by drawing an arbitrary and therefore exclusionary boundary around it. Perhaps a better strategy is to create an opportunity to stimulate individual, self-directed channels of inquiry, by way of asking a few key questions:

— What do we human beings truly need in order to be healthy in mind, body, and spirit?

— What can go wrong when we do not get what we truly need?

— In what ways, if any, do women's fundamental needs differ from men's? What ways do men's needs differ from women's?

— To what degree are our basic needs genetically determined versus culturally determined?

— What do children really need from their parents? From their culture? What happens when they receive something less?

— Where do our values come from? Which values serve to satisfy our fundamental needs, which only distract us from these needs?

— What is truth, what is not truth, and how can we tell the difference? Is truth absolute, relative, or some combination of the two?

— What constitutes happiness? How can we achieve it?

In addition to pondering these questions, you might also wish to read through the "Daily Reminders" litany at the end of this book, pausing after each reminder to ask yourself two questions: Is what is being said here true? How (where) can I find out?

Again, the purpose of these questions is to provoke you into engaging in a self-directed reading program to enrich your overall context of understanding—of what it means to be fully human—from a common point of view.

Tips. The following tips for engaging in a self-directed reading program are intended in particular for minimal or resistant readers. However, even avid readers, especially those whose harried lives find them compelled to be breathlessly in many places at once, may find them useful:

— Focus on only one reading (book, article) at a time; avoid accumulating a library of nagging guilt (see *Glossary*).

— Set aside (and commit yourself to) a daily reading time, even if it's only a modest one; for example, consider going to bed a half-hour earlier than usual, or reading a few pages at your desk just after lunch.

— Start your reading program out on a quota basis, beginning with a limit of just a few pages (three of four) each day, strictly adhered to. Then increase your quota only if and when you are motivated by "want to" rather than "ought to." In other words, you make the rules.

— Build positive associations into your reading time by complementing it with such things as playing relaxing music, sitting under a warming sun, or sipping a steaming cup of tea or coffee. Baby yourself.

— If you need "transition time," take a short walk or a warm shower before you sit down to read; you may even wish to use this time to think about what you last read.

— Write notes in the page margins as you read; speak to what is spoken. Question everything. Make associations with your own experience. If you think the author is being thoughtlessly obtuse (a problem more common than is admitted to), tell the author off!

— If possible, discuss what you read with someone of kindred interest. Discourse is midwife to the thoughts and ideas gestating in the womb of our unconscious.

— If you can't get into a book, put it aside and pick up another. Avoid "toughing it out" simply as a way of avoiding "failure."

— Consider joining a mail-order book club, such as the Quality Paperback Library, especially if going to the library or bookstore is likely to be "one more thing."

• **Observing**

The other means, or tool, we all have at out disposal for enriching our overall context of understanding is observing.

Do you ever wonder who originates all those jokes we hear at work that make us laugh because they reflect in caricature a basic truth about ourselves? Well, we have a pretty good idea of who these invisible geniuses are not, don't we? We know, for instance, that they aren't the kind of people who are always rehearsing what they're going to say all the while they're barely pretending to listen to what we have to say. And we know they aren't the kind of people who, like political or religious fundamentalists, don't need to look any further to answer questions because they've already found all the answers. And we know they aren't the kind of people who walk past the janitor in their office building without making eye contact; or who jog down tree-shaded sidewalks with a walkman jammed in their ears. These people aren't observers of others.

Fundamentally, we gather information in two basic ways: (1) Indirectly, by reading about and/or listening to the life experiences, observations, and notions of others; (2) directly, by observing and/or experiencing life firsthand. Most of us use some combination of these; however, as suggested earlier, at least some of us are naturally inclined to favor one over the other. Whatever our inclination, though, direct observation and experience is an essential part of gaining general knowledge about human nature and the human condition, serving as a primary source of information and as a means of confirming or validating information gathered by other means.

Observation is only effective, however, to the degree we observe purely and unselectively. We must restrain ourselves from filtering what we observe through latent biases and fears, and we must restrain ourselves from irrationally excluding possible sources of information. Indeed, who among us has not paid a terrible price after falling into the trap of seeing only what we want to see, only what is "safe" to see, only what is confirming of what we already know ?

Effective observation requires not only the active participation of all our senses, including our listening ears, but also the active participation of our rational, probing minds. Indeed, it is not enough simply to watch people in motion, as we might watch actors in a play; it is also necessary to ask why these people are in motion in the particular ways that they are:

— Why is this person behaving the way she is? What's driving her?

— Where does this drive come from?

— Is this person's behavior healthy? Is it "normal"—widely shared by others?

— Is this behavior genetically based or culturally based? Or is it some combination of these?

— Is this person fully aware of what she is doing and therefore making a fully conscious decision to do it? If not, who or what is making this decision?

— Do I behave in the same or a similar way, or entirely differently? In either case, why do I?

Effective observation is inclusive—not limited to the behavior of our too-oft-anthropocentric Homo sapien selves. It allows for a full and unrestricted opportunity to observe patterns, draw parallels, and discover connections among all living things, along the full continuum of our common being. Indeed, we can truly enrich our context of understanding only to the degree we supplement objective observations of our own kind with close observations of kindred others, from near cousins such as macaques and African dogs to more-distant cousins such as ants and honey bees.

At a minimum, expanding the scope of our observations in this way can greatly deepen our appreciation for the complexity of behavior among all social (group-oriented) creatures, and help us sort out which kinds of behaviors are strongly genetically based and which are strongly culturally based. It can also help us understand and appreciate what an enormous risk Mother Nature took when she loosed the reins of strict behavioral programming to create what we call "free will."

Needless to say, there is one other subject we should include in our observations—ourselves. In fact, observing (rather than judging) ourselves can be a great way of developing a keen sense of humor.

A final word before we move on: The process of building a context of understanding and striving to gain the capacity to exercise compassion—even in the most difficult of situations, will likely be lengthy—perhaps even lifelong. It will require commitment, energy, courage, forbearance, sacrifice, and resolve. The good news is that the Universal Law of Personal Investing applies: The more you invest of yourself now, when the opportunity for growth is greatest, the greater will be the aggregate of your rewards down the road.

Forgiving

We now come to the heart of the matter, though there are certainly plenty of earnest dissenters out there who will tell us we have not come to the heart of the matter at all—that forgiveness, the exercise of unconditional compassion toward those damaged human beings in our lives who in turn damaged us, is not the heart of the matter at all. They will tell us that if we are incest survivors, we are under no obligation whatsoever to even consider, even for a single moment forgiving the "son of a bitch" who raped us and betrayed what is the perhaps most sacred of all trusts. Or, if we are Jewish, they will tell us that we are under no obligation whatsoever to forgive those "evil Nazi monsters"—or their heirs—who exterminated or otherwise brutalized millions of our kindred. Or, if we are black, they will tell us we never have to forgive those "honky racist" white people for breaking our individual and collective spirit, for robbing us of all but the very last drop of our self-esteem and our will to hope. And they are right—up to a point.

The incontestable, undeniable, inviolable truth is this: No one on this earth is under any obligation—moral, legal, social, ethical, or otherwise—to forgive anybody for anything. Anymore than any of us is under an obligation—moral, social, ethical, or otherwise—to smile at everyone she meets. However, this is not the issue at hand: We are not talking about "obligations" here—of biblical or any other proportion: We are not talking about appeasing an angry, all-seeing, all-judging parent-god. We are talking about "getting on with it"—about what we all, without exception, have to do (but are not obligated to do). No matter what our particular circumstance—who we are or what has been done to us—we must free ourselves of the fierce gravity of an ego self grown massive with unresolved pain and anger. This pain and anger grows invisible tentacles that keep us stuck in the past, and (to once again mix our metaphors) it produces sulfurous rain that poisons our soul, preventing us from growing the fruits of ultimate fulfillment in our garden within.

We are unquestionably free, utterly free, to choose not to forgive those who have "trespassed" against us. This choice is as much an inalienable right for every individual as is life, liberty, or the pursuit of happiness. But it comes with an inescapable cost, potentially a very dear one. Indeed, we can get through life without forgiving those who have trespassed against us, just as we can get through another day (aided by perhaps an aspirin or two) bearing another migraine; however, we cannot fully engage in it, cannot fully revel in it, cannot fully exult in it. We cannot fully participate in all that life is or can be. We cannot be full partners in our own miraculous becoming. We can never experience that deep inner peace that can only come, like a soft summer breeze, to the soul that is free of all bitterness and grief, that is free of any consuming need for "just compensation," that is open to honoring the common miracle of our mutual being.

> **Note:** If you find yourself resistant to the prospect of forgiving certain individuals in your past or present life, or if you are confused about what forgiveness asks of you, you may wish to ponder certain notions about forgiveness before going any further down the present path. Here are a two resources you may find helpful in this regard: Robin Casarjian"s *Forgiveness: A Bold*

Choice for a Peaceful Heart (Bantam Books, 1992), and Chapter 12 ("Marking Territory: The Boundaries of Rage and Forgiveness") in Clarissa Pinkola Estés' *Women Who Run With the Wolves* (see "Suggested Readings") Ponder what these authors, as well as others, have to say about forgiveness. You may also wish to ponder why Christ was so preoccupied with the notion of forgiving "those who have trespassed against us." Go slow, since certain things simply cannot, and should not, be rushed.

Our Goal

Even though the heart of the matter is indeed forgiveness, this does not mean we must accomplish it before we can do anything else, or that we must accomplish it all at once, as if by god-like decree: "As of this instant, I forgive all of you for all your transgressions for all time. Go in peace." Nor must we accomplish it completely.

Forgiveness is an essential part of any process for getting on with it, but it is no more essential or preeminent than any other part. We can get to forgiveness through the front door, the back door, a downstairs window—even through an attic window. Forgiveness is not a fully formed something, like a gift item we might buy from a quaint shop and then choose either to grant or to withhold as whim or fancy may suit us. Forgiveness is both a *goal* and a *process*—a state of being and an act of becoming. We forgive by being and by becoming compassionate—ultimately, unconditionally compassionate.

Forgiveness is hard work. For some of us, it may seem so daunting and impossible, that we may feel we are not yet ready for it. We may even feel we'll never be ready for it. If this is true for you, there is no need to be concerned or to feel left out or inadequate. Again, there are no obligations and no rules, other than the one universal rule that each of us recognize and follow her own truth, not whatever might be true for the other person. If the mere suggestion that you begin a process toward forgiving a "monster" in your life feels like a command from an overbearing authority figure to place your hand on a hot burner or to make "Sophie's Choice," then you need to heed this feeling and choose accordingly. Hopefully, you will choose in such a way that does not shut you off from any possibility of revisiting this issue later in your journey.

Our goal, then, is not to forgive by decree, but simply to engage in a process that leads us toward unconditional compassion.

The Process

Any process toward forgiveness must ultimately be an individual one, tailored to fit who we are in the moment. There are four major tasks, however, that are probably essential to any such process, irrespective of how we might go about accomplishing them:

- Acknowledging the harm done to us

- Embracing our pain and anger

- Grieving for what has been lost

- Letting go of the child within

Acknowledging the harm done to us. For many of us, acknowledging the harm done to us, especially harm done to us by our parents, is not a simple matter of pulling the rug off all those elephants that the family has been hiding under the carpet in the living room all these years. If only it could be that simple—that we could just reach out and grab a hold of that rug and give it a good yank.

Before we can actually pull on that rug, we must first be willing to admit there is something under it to be uncovered ("What lumps?"), and then we must be wholly willing to uncover it. In other words, we must be willing to come face to face with a reality that our demon fear within may tell us is a forbidden fruit from the Tree of Knowledge. If we pick this fruit, we would be subjecting ourselves to unimaginable, unbearable horrors.

As children, most of us needed to place our parents on one of the highest pedestals in the pantheon of our heroes. We did this because we needed to expect more of them than we could expect of ourselves or others. We needed our parents to be as powerful and as good as we could possibly make them so that we could feel as safe and secure as the limits of fantasy would allow. Indeed, the higher we could manage to place our parents on a pedestal and the more god-like we could make them, the safer and more cherished we made ourselves feel.

As adults, many of us, despite all that has happened to us, tend to continue to keep our parents on that pedestal. We do this for at least three very good reasons:

1. There is a natural momentum to the realities we construct or participate in when we are children, and the more important these realities are to us, the less likely we are to do anything to diminish them.

2. As long as we can sustain a childlike reverence for our parents, whether they deserve such reverence or not, we can continue to protect ourselves from facing any ugly, perhaps painful truths about them.

3. To acknowledge that our parents have deep-seated flaws, some likely genetic, would be to risk having to acknowledge the same intrinsic flaws (and inevitable fate) in ourselves: "Like parent, like. . . ."

How do we manage to do this? As our parents are failing us, perhaps even inflicting great physical or emotional injury on us, how do we manage to overcome a paradox of perhaps glaring proportions and keep our parents perched on that pedestal? In other words, what alchemy do we employ to transform agents of harm into angels of love?

The human psyche is expedient to whatever we believe we need in order to survive. Indeed, some of us resolved this perhaps glaring paradox by simply appropriating our parents' failures as our own: We assumed that what our parents did to us, or failed to do, could not possibly be their fault and therefore had to be our fault. In other words, we elevated our parents to such a height that the only flaws remaining within view were glaringly those staring back at us in the mirror every day. This strategy, or sleight of mind, came especially easily to many of us, because its archetype had very early on been indelibly etched into our psyche by the parent-child model presented in the Old and New Testaments: Just as the angry, vindictive "Father" of the Bible had a right to punish his "fallen" or "sinful" children, so did our parents have a right to "punish" their undeserving children however they saw fit.

Some of us went so far as to deny away one whole side of this seeming paradox (the agent of harm side) in favor of the other (the angel of love side), using a convenient control trick that in essence elevates us to godliness: By refusing to acknowledge something, by denying it, we could keep it from being true—from existing. In essence, we edited from our consciousness, from our "Swiss cheese" memory, all our parents' failings, and all the painful consequences of these failures. We inflicted ourselves with a sort of selective amnesia, and, in so doing, created our own selective reality.

The costs owing to our defying the law of gravity and playing god have been, and continue to be, several and onerous. Of these, exhaustion is perhaps the most palpable, especially if we have reached middle age. Indeed, it takes an enormous amount of energy to keep elevated that which Truth's gravity is constantly threatening to bring crashing to our feet. It takes even more energy to construct and constantly edit our own reality, our own little universe.

Perhaps the single greatest cost we have inflicted on ourselves, though, has been the loss of past opportunities of discovering, and eventually dealing with, the root cause of the seeming eternity of our discontent. In maintaining a false reality, we have denied ourselves both the opportunity and the energy to acknowledge fully and completely the extent to which we have been damaged by the very mortals we have been attempting all these years to transfigurate into angels.

Although some of us have indeed begun a process of discovery and acknowledgment, many more of us have not, or we are only in the very early stages. Wherever you might be in such a process, you might wish to use the following technique to facilitate it: write down, or commit to tape, *everything* you can remember in regard to injuries inflicted on you by intimate others. Record all the shaming, the exploitation, the neglect, the manipulation, the deep wounding—*all* of it.

You may be resistant to doing this. After all, why should you so formally put yourself through something so potentially unpleasant? The reason is simple, but significant: There is a very large difference between merely thinking about something in the abstract (and thereby minimizing its reality) and giving this same something both form and voice (and thereby allowing it the fullness of its reality). To appreciate this difference, visualize the color red in your mind (or an elephant hiding under the living room rug). Now look directly at any object within your view that is colored red (or, if you happened to have one around, an elephant standing in full stature). There is indeed a very large difference between the two, is there not—between the ephemeral lingering of something in the abstract and the incarnation of the same something in the flesh, so to speak? Indeed, when we keep our thoughts and memories, and therefore our feelings about these thoughts and feelings, in the realm of the abstract, we are able to maintain our almost absol   ￢n-trol over them, to keep them slavishly susceptible and pliant to muscled powers of denial. When we put them down on par￢ however, we are in essence releasing our iron hold over acknowledging their existence—giving birth to them. We are also giving birth to ourselves.

But it is not without pain. Indeed, pain is an inevitable, perhaps even essential, part of any transformation (as symbolized by Christ's transformation on the cross: dying in the secular in order to be born in the spiritual). In writing or taping it all down, we are inevitably, unavoidably, inescapably going to encounter some very powerful emotions—not simply anger, but rage; not simply pain, but agony. The reason for this is that, just as suppressing or denying away a truth does not make this truth go away, suppressing or denying away the emotion triggered by this truth does not make this emotion go away. Like credit card debt, our denial only delays and accumulates it. This leads us to the next step in our progression toward making peace with the past: embracing our pain and anger.

Embracing our pain and anger. As we noted immediately above, fully acknowledging the betrayals and injuries inflicted on us when we were children is likely to unleash some very powerful emotions in us. These feelings may be so powerful, in fact, that we may be inclined to hide from them, just as we might be inclined to bury our heads under the covers as sharp claps of thunder inevitably follow blinding flashes of lightning. Instead of trying to avoid these perhaps overwhelming emotions, however, we must do the exact opposite: We must wrap our arms right around them and embrace them wholly, squeeze them tightly, feel them fully—so that we can then let go of them. There is no other way.

And there is no easy way. For one thing, it takes a great deal of courage—the kind it takes to get ourselves to a doctor when we discover a lump in our breast. ("It's not really there; I just imagined it.") In addition, for many of us, it requires that we give ourselves permission to defy certain messages we internalized in our unquestioning youth concerning the "badness" of strong emotions: "It's wrong to hate"..."It's not ladylike to be angry"..."Real men don't cry". Unfortunately, this permission, even though it needs only come from within, can be very difficult for us to grant. It can be as difficult, for instance, as choosing *not* to go out of our way to avoid another intimidating "authority figure." If, however, we can take a few steps back from ourselves (from our fearful child selves), we may better see that ·ch messages are not only patently absurd, defying all logic, they are counterproductive to normal human functioning. Indeed, why would Nature have gone to the trouble of giving us these emotions, carefully developing and enriching them over the eons, if she did not intend for us to feel them, to express them, to use them toward our continued survival and well-being?

Viewed within the context of the whole, rage, hate, and anger (see *Glossary*) are every bit as natural and essential to our overall well-being and humanity as are joy, love, and compassion. And they are all—anger as well as joy, hate as well as love—equally and wholly value-neutral: they are neither inherently negative or inherently positive, neither inherently "bad" or inherently "good." It is only when we act on an emotion, and must therefore take into consideration the effect our action might have on others, that we need to assign relative values, negative or positive, "bad" or "good." Feeling is free, acting is not.

Before you begin the exercise suggested in the previous section (which you may wish to put in the form of a letter directed toward a particular person), you may wish to consciously declare total freedom from any need to censor your words; any need to edit your memories or your thoughts; or any need to exercise any understanding or compassion (at this point).

In doing this exercise, your sole purpose is to fully acknowledge every betrayal of trust committed against you, every injurious act inflicted upon you, every selfish manipulation foisted on you. It is also to fully embrace and feel every emotion consequent to these misdeeds and omissions—as consequent as heat is to fire.

The very last thing you want to be doing at this point is holding anything back. To further help you in this regard, you may wish to follow these additional guidelines:

- **Before writing or taping, remember that no thought or feeling, acknowledged only to one's self, can ever do anyone any harm; likewise, no word or phrase, expressed only in one's own company, can ever do anyone any harm.**

  No lightning bolt is going to strike us dead for expressing the truth that dwells in our minds, our hearts, or our souls. No deity worth our honor and respect would ever punish us for acknowledging the truth as we are able to see, feel, or sense it, or for expressing this truth in whatever terms or passions are necessary to fully acknowledge it.

The truth sets us free. Never does it, nor can it, condemn us. It is ignorance and denial—it is fear—that condemns us.

- **Avoid writing or taping your letter when or where there is any chance you might be interrupted and thereby placed in a position in which you might be or feel pressured to explain what you are doing to someone who does not need to know.**

This does not mean that absolutely no one should know what you are intending to do. For example, if you are in individual or group therapy, you may wish to share your intentions—but not the results of your intentions—with your therapist or with your fellow group members. Again, this letter is for your eyes (and soul) only. If you make it otherwise, you will almost certainly end up censoring what you put down on paper (even before you put it down), or otherwise holding back, and thereby diminishing the power of this potentially very valuable exercise.

Indeed, if you are one of those many of us who has trouble establishing and maintaining boundaries, here perhaps is a good opportunity to get a little practice.

- **Address your letter to a specific person, even when the real target of your letter is an institution (for example, an orga- nized religion, in which case you might direct your letter toward a prelate who symbolizes or represents this institu- tion).**

Directing your letter toward a specific person can be an effec- tive way of keeping the contents of your letter honest and sharply focused, as opposed to avoidive and self-protectively general. In other words, it can help keep you speaking in the active rather than the passive voice. For example, you are more likely to say something like, "You were always criticizing me, you sonuvabitch! Never once did you ever praise me...for anything. Not once!" than something flaccid like, "I was always being crit- icized, never praised".

Note, too, that this strategy tends to affix responsibility (blame) where it belongs—with the adult perpetrator, rather than with the confused child still within you. Indeed, holding a particular face in mind as you write can be just the "seed water" you need to pump long-suppressed memories and feelings to the surface.

If you do choose to address a specific person, keep in mind that it is not your intention at this point to actually deliver what you say (or how you say it) to the person you are addressing. At this early stage it is only your intention to fully acknowledge the truth as you perceive it, and to fully express the feelings inextricably and painfully associated this truth.

- **Once you start writing or taping, write or speak as freely and rapidly as you can.**

Pausing is an opportunity to judge what we are saying and therefore to censor it. It also diminishes or interrupts the flow from the wellspring of memories and feelings pent-up deep within us. Avoid it. Keep pen to paper. Allow yourself unrestricted freedom to free-associate: to conjure one memory, thought, or feeling and let it trigger another, that memory, thought, or feeling to trigger another; and so on. This is not a time or place to be concerned with the "correctness" of your grammar, the acceptability of your language, or the ferocity of your feelings.

If you are more comfortable expressing yourself with drawings than with words, then by all means do so. However, again, it is important to keep moving, to avoid pausing in order to pass judgment on the aesthetics or acceptability of your work.

- **Write (or speak) in shorthand, hieroglyphics, four-letter words, right-to-left, top-to-bottom—however you need to in the moment.**

As you scribble your thoughts and feelings down on paper (or tape)—in words, pictures, or whatever—avoid getting hung up in standards, conventions, rules, correctness, aesthetics, form, or guilt. No one is going to judge either what you say or how you say it. In other words, allow yourself complete freedom to intermix feeling with form, form with feeling. If you need to stab the paper with your pencil, stab it—stab the hell out of it. Feel free to crunch your writing paper into a ball and throw it against the wall, or to flush your recording tape down the toilet.

There are as many ways to express ourselves as there are needs for expression. And there is nothing inherently "wrong" with any one of them, as long as no one else is involved; they are all as value-neutral as are the thoughts and feelings they express.

- **Dispose of your letter or tape as soon as you are able to let go of it.**

Even though your letter or tape is specifically directed toward a particular person, it is actually intended for your eyes (or ears) only. In its present form, it is entirely private and should never, under any circumstances, be seen or heard by anyone else, not even by your closest friend or your therapist. This letter or tape is part of a process only just begun. It is a first draft, and no one, not even the most accomplished of writers or composers, ever shows or otherwise exposes to public view their first drafts.

After you are ready to let go of your letter or tape, consider burning it as opposed to simply placing it in the trash, where it might inadvertently be found by someone not as far along in their journey toward unconditional compassion as you are.

- **Repeat this exercise as often as you need to, and for as many "audiences" as you need to address.**

Avoid trying to rush toward a complete acknowledgment of all the harm that was done to you. Like all masterpieces, it simply will not be rushed. In fact, you may find that you will need to write or tape raging letters to the same person several times before you finally get it all out.

Of course, if more than one person did you harm, you will have to direct separate, and perhaps multiple, letters or tapes, toward each person involved. Take your time; be patient—let the process control itself.

Unfortunately, there is an unavoidable cost or consequence to doing what we have now had the courage to do, and we must now come to grips with this consequence. When we acknowledge all the terrible harm done to us and fully acknowledge what has been irrestorably stolen from us, we leave behind a hole, a vacuum, of perhaps crushing proportions. We experience a death for which we must now grieve.

Grieving for what has been lost. The letters we write to fully acknowledge the harm done to us, and to fully express our rage and pain, are, at bottom, an acknowledgment of irretrievable loss. In giving form and voice to the truth about the damage and its source, we are giving form and voice to another truth:

- A great portion of our life—perhaps an entire childhood— has forever been lost.

- The wounded child-within (see *Glossary*) we've been so tenaciously hanging onto will never be rescued, will never be loved unconditionally by pedestaled angels.

- All those unhappy memories inextricably associated with gut-wrenching loneliness, shame, abandonment, and self-loathing will never be supplanted by an idyllic picture album of our own choosing. Indeed, we are finally acknowledging that what might have been can simply never be, and that it is time now for us to grieve for our loss- to weep for the child within, the child who never was and can never be, the child we have too long been hanging onto.

Much has been written in the popular literature in recent years about "healing" (see *Glossary*) the child within. Almost nothing, however, has been written about grieving for the child within—letting go. This is unfortunate (but understandable in a culture that is alienated from death) and is perhaps one of the reasons many of us have gotten stuck in our efforts to get on with our lives: Attempting to heal a part of us that can never be made whole, restored, or "made right" tends to focus us narrowly on a particularly seductive image (a helpless, abandoned waif, limp in our arms). This in turn diverts energy and resolve we might otherwise use in doing the hard work we must all do, sooner or later, to heal the adult within us. Indeed, what most of us need to do at this point in our troubled lives is not to heal the child within, but simply to let go of her—to grieve for her: *To every thing there is a season, and a time to every purpose under the heaven. A time to be born, and a time to die. A time to weep...a time to mourn.*

We should not, however, do our mourning in a dark corner off by ourselves, in compliance with some inherited script that compels that we bear our grief in heroic anonymity or be forever shamed. Whatever messages about stoicism or broad shoulders or fierce independence or stiff upper lips we might have received during our formative years, the truth is that the four-and-a-half billion years of evolution that forged us into the highly social, highly interdependent beings did not prepare us to grieve for our losses entirely within the slender shadow of our own company. Indeed, the very opposite is true. The whole underlying purpose of the wake, funeral, and memorial service—despite how hollow and ineffectual these formal rituals have become in our thoroughly cynicized, secularized, alienated culture—was to provide a mutually supportive context for mutually unabashed mourning.

Grieving is a time to be in the close, caring company of like others. It is a time to seek out kindred souls to weep with, to vent with, to talk with, to simply be with. We have fully acknowledged the harm done to us: This is what happened to me. We have embraced our pain and anger: And you did it, you bastard! Now it is time for us to grieve for what has been irretrievably lost: There's a sucking hole at the very center of my soul.

Of course, we are not privileged to turn our grief on or off by a flick of a button, as we do with so many other things in this gadgetized world of ours, so we cannot and should not confine our grieving to only those hours when we are in caring, supportive company. Friends and caring others can help us carry our load. They can salve the wound in our soul with extra love and generosity until it begins to close and heal. However, they cannot carry the whole load for us. Some part of our grief we simply must bear alone, under our own strength. Even so, we should make the effort to share our grief with supportive people to the extent possible. In turn, we should share their grief. Giving and receiving comfort can move us well beyond mere catharsis. Indeed, is there any power on this earth more transforming and miraculous in its powers than a hug received or given when it is most needed? Here are suggestions designed to help you with your own grieving process:

- **Use an old photograph of you as a child to help you focus your grief.**
  Many people in our culture are appalled (are made uncomfortable, at the very least) by the tradition of publicly displaying the body of a dead fellow human being; they think this a barbaric, if not downright macabre, thing to do. However, there is a deep logic behind this ancient ritual: The tangible presence of a deceased loved one serves to confront us with our grief and force

it to the surface. The presence of fellow grievers serves to give us permission to unabashedly purge ourselves of our grief.

In less emotionally constipated cultures, men and women even go so far as to throw themselves on the body of a deceased loved one and wail as if possessed by the furies of Hades. These people are not "making fools out of themselves," as some in our culture might adjudge. They are getting it all out, wholly and efficiently, so they can get on with their lives. In fact, many people in this world simply do not have the luxury of preoccupying themselves with their grief while all else waits. They either get on with it or they (or intimate others) perish.

We are programmed to respond emotionally to the concrete, not to the abstract. Hence, just as we can use an embalmed body to stimulate our grief over the loss of a loved one, so might we also use an old yellowed photograph to stimulate our grief over the loss of a part of ourselves—our childhood. Dig out an old baby picture of yourself and see what happens.

In fact, at the appropriate time, you may wish to take this photograph to where you grew up as a child and bury it (or a copy) in a place that holds particular significance for you. You will know exactly the right place. (The author's was beneath a chestnut tree whose shady and "armed" branches had held the tree fort the author had used as a safe place throughout his preteens. This tree fort had since served as a metaphor to him for physical and emotional safety.)

- **Consider joining a facilitated therapy group, the local Alanon or ACOA group, or some other such support group.**

Part of the deep logic that underlies the wake ritual also underlies the old adage "misery loves company," and we need to pay attention to this logic. Though it is certainly true that misery sometimes seeks out like company simply to justify and perpetuate itself, more often it is to secure a context in which it can freely and fully express itself, and thereby fulfill itself. Indeed, the misery of our grief remains unfulfilled—short of "doing its thing"—until it runs its full course.

Consider taking your grief to the company of like grievers. Be prepared to comfort as well as to be comforted.

- **Prepare to experience at least some degree of depression during your mourning period.**

Depression is our psyche's self-protective response to loss and its sometimes unbearable pain. It helps dull our senses until the worst of the sting that comes with loss has dissipated. Therefore, it can be very helpful, even lifesaving, protecting us from potentially damaging extremes. However, if we are not vigilant, depression can become a sort of opiate we use to protect ourselves from feeling anything at all, other than perhaps self-pity, thereby removing any stimulus for getting on with it. (Some of us suffer a chronic form of depression that serves this purpose.)

In dealing with depression, you may wish to assume the following attitude: Yes, a little depression can be good for me—a shot of Novocaine to see me through the worst of the drilling—but I will not use it to avoid the hard work of extricating myself from its fierce hold. If necessary, I will seek out professional help. At the very least, I will let others take me by the hand and lead me to such help.

Letting go. We have acknowledged the harm done to us, we have embraced our pain and anger, and we have grieved for what has been irretrievably lost. Now, finally, it is time to let go. Now it is time to forgive.

There are probably as many ways to let go, to forgive, as there are ways to rationalize not letting go. Whatever way you ultimately choose will depend on your particular situation, and on who you are in the moment. Only you can know and decide which way is best. One way to let go is simply to pursue to its natural conclusion the process you already have begun: Concretely declaring your sentiments on paper, as opposed to keeping them perhaps safely held in the elusive abstract. If we can commit words of forgiveness to paper and bring ourselves to make these words physically real (actual red as opposed to abstract red), we will at the same time make them, at least in part, emotionally real (truly felt), and spiritually real (truly liberating).

If you choose to declare your forgiveness on paper, write another draft of the letter you wrote as a way of fully acknowledging all the harm that was done to you. This time, though, take out all the residual words of blame and rage. Make this letter your "masterpiece."

- **First, take a deep breath and hold it just long enough to make yourself aware of the muscles holding onto the toxic air being trapped in your lungs. Then let go of it.**

As you relax the diaphragm with which you hold onto your breath, likewise relax the deeper diaphragm with which you may be holding onto any residual anger and pain.

- **Take stock: Are you truly ready to let go?**

If so, sharpen your pencil or put a fresh tape into your recorder. If not, pass by this place for now, with possible intent of revisiting it at a later point. Can it ever be too late to return? No. Never. There are no distancing straight lines where you are now; there are only circles. Circles upon circles. (In truth, you will inevitably return here whether you presently intend to or not!)

- **Direct this new draft of your letter to the same person to whom you directed the earlier, wholly uninhibited, thoroughly purgative one.**

In this version of your letter, as you similarly did in the earlier one, tell this person how he or she has harmed you and how all the resultant damage has affected (limited) your life; tell this person what he or she has irretrievably taken away from you. However, avoid using any language that is either blaming, damning, punishing, or vindictive. Simply state the facts (this is the way it was; this is the way it is) as if you were a third party writing or speaking about someone else.

Now tell this person that you understand they would not have done these painful things to you had they not been similarly inflicted with pain in their own life, probably during their own childhood. If you are aware of any specific incidents or facts about this person's own childhood that support your compassionate view, include them here. Especially powerful would be any incident showing this person being treated exactly as he or she has treated you.

At the very end of your letter, write down or say the single most powerful phrase any language can express: I forgive you. If there are still tears, let them flow. These are healing tears—raindrops on your garden within.

- **If appropriate, actually deliver your message to the intended person.**

After writing or taping your letter of letting go, you may feel a need to actually deliver your message to the person for whom it is intended, even if this person is no longer available to you. If this is the case, proceed slowly: Let your letter rest for a while, preferably for at least a week or two, then go back to it and reread it to ensure that it is truly an unrippled surface reflecting a truly compassionate heart. Don't be surprised if the otherwise serene surface of your letter still contains a ripple or two of lingering, resolved anger. If this is the case, you may still have some work to do. Be patient. Some things cannot be hurried, and getting to forgiveness, truly letting go, is one of them.

If the person to whom you feel a need to actually deliver your letter is no longer available to you (deceased, for example), you can still deliver your letter—symbolically. For example, if the intended person is no longer living, you might take your letter to their grave site and either read or paraphrase your letter out loud or perhaps bury it in a plastic bag beside their headstone, or both. Or, you might take your letter to a session with your therapist or your therapy group and read it out loud to them (or ask someone else to read it for you). Or, you might take your letter back to where you grew up as a child and leave it in a place that has special significance for you. (Caution: If you choose to bury or leave your letter somewhere, be sure there is no return address on it, in order to protect yourself from anyone who may inadvertently discover your letter and may not be as far along on their spiritual path as you are.)

Your letter has to be uniquely your own, of course, but sometimes an example can be helpful as a guide, and perhaps as a bit of a motivator. The following letter, sealed in a plastic freezer bag, is buried at the foot of a pinkish headstone in Northern New York.

Dear Dad,

How strange it still feels to address you as
"Dad"—you were always a stranger to me. And how
terribly empty our estrangement still makes me
feel.

Although I am not very good at expressing myself
in face-to-face encounters, without benefit of
being able to carefully compose, and to edit, I do
wish I were face-to-face with you now, so I could
tell you in person everything I have so long needed to tell you. Perhaps that's what paradise is—
being able to sit in perfect intimacy, by an
unhurried stream on a butterfly-filled afternoon,
and tell each other everything we've always needed
to tell each other, and be heard with absolute
acceptance,

I did try telling you once, though—remember? It
was just after my senior year at college. I had
failed to graduate with my class, because I'd
flunked a required German course, for the second
time. I had arrived home an utter dissipant, weighing over 260 pounds, and looking it. And my arrogance—I thought they'd let me graduate no matter
what, because I was such a Big Man on Campus- had
robbed you of my help at the marina that summer,
because I was going to have to make up the German
course in summer school, if I were to go on to
Cornell in the fall, to become the second in the
family to get into an Ivy League law school. In
the face of all this, all this shame, this utter
shame, you had said not one word to me, either of
consolation or of punishment. The excruciating
silence was more than I could bear.

One night, I have forgotten why, I suddenly
erupted at the supper table, that rack and pinion
of so many other humiliations over the years, and
poured my heart out to you. I went and on,
gushing uncharacteristically, without benefit of

careful composition or editing, for what seemed like hours but was probably only a few minutes. At the end of it all, when I had finally reached exhaustion, you said nothing. Not a single word. You simply got up from the table, as if nothing out of the ordinary had occurred, nothing had been said, and hurried off to your marina, your lee harbor, and left me sitting in the warm liquid of my own regret, my own humiliation, feeling as if I had just peed my pants in front of the whole world. In the excruciating agony of that terrible moment, I wanted to die.

But I did not—either then or in any of the many other black moments of bottomless despair I have known since. And this letter is one more measure to ensure that I not, until it is my time, for there is so very, very much work I must do yet, including getting at least a good start at repairing all the damage I have caused, both in act and in omission, while blinded by, preoccupied with, my own pain. Here, then, is what I need to say to you, not as a way of blaming you, or of punishing you, but simply as a way of letting you go, so that I might get on with doing the work I now feel I was intended to do—to break the cycle. For both of us:

As my father, my validator, you never once told me that you loved me; never once gave me a hug, squeezed my hand, or patted me on the back. You never once read me a bedtime story or took me on an "adventure," just the two of us. You never once told me I played a good game, even when I came close, or congratulated me on any of my achievements, all of which I did just for you, to show you that I was "good enough" after all. You never once shared with me even a single story about your own childhood, or gave me benefit of your fatherly wisdom.

When I graduated from high school as valedicto-

rian of my class, forewent a normal adolescence in
order to make you proud, you said nothing. When I
built sleek, silvery rockets, risked life and limb
to blast them masterfully into the sky, you said
nothing. When I swam across the frigid, heat-suck-
ing waters of Lake Ontario, crawled through the
last three miles with a ruptured lung, you said
nothing. When I helped you build your marina,
ripped four fingernails off my right hand wrestling
one of the massive timbers of the monument of your
"success," you said nothing. When I willed myself
through the relentless agony of Navy SEAL training,
fated myself to the quagmires of Vietnam while
other fathers' sons were fleeing off to Canada, you
said nothing.

And so it has always been, and so it still is:
your silence, in life as well as in death, making
me feel that nothing I do, nothing I sacrifice,
nothing I achieve, is ever quite good enough; making me view every success as a failure; making me
to try ever harder to attain what, in truth, no
human being could ever possibly attain.

The size of your huge hand still looms large in
my dreams, the sausage-sized fingers, the postage-
stamp nails. When you spanked me with it, you hit
me so hard, so without restraint, so without end,
I thought you wanted me dead, to never have been
born. The murderous rage in your eyes became the
demons of my dreams, haunting me, tormenting me,
even to this very day. You made me live in fear of
you, your presence, the mere anticipation of your
presence. You made me feel that I deserved such
punishment, such torture, that there was something
inherently wrong with me, that I was deficient or
"bad." You made me feel that everybody would be
much better off, including myself, if I were no
longer around.

I needed you to love me, I needed you to vali-
date me, I needed you to bless me, I needed you to

accept me—just as I was. Instead, you rejected me, you abandoned me, you punished me, you cast me into a living hell of relentless, gnawing self-loathing and utter aloneness. You made me feel insignificant, you made me feel unlovable, you made me feel unworthy, you made me feel ashamed. You caused me to want out, to fantasize out, to contemplate out, to scheme out. Thank God, though, I did not choose out, despite stepping up to the very brink more than once. Was it your hand that held me back? I am now ready to entertain such notions, however remote their possibility.

I do so wish you were here with me in the flesh, in the moment, so I could put my arms around you now and give you a big hug, and tell you that I understand that you did not mean to hurt me, any more than I have meant to hurt any of my own children, which I most certainly have done. Though I know very little about your life, I do know you were driven by a deep sense of humiliation.

I forgive you, Dad. I forgive you all of it, I do not need to hang on to all the hurt anymore, nor do I need to hang on to any impossible dreams about what might have been, the childhood lost. You have taken much from me, but you also have gifted me with much, including the courage and the resolve to slay the demon dragon of our common legacy, which I shall now set about doing, with all my energy, for the sake of all our children, the "seven generations" to come.

May you now, and forever, rest in peace. It was not your fault. It was nobody's fault. It just was.

Love . . . .

Sometimes, instead of a single, tangible person, an entire, faceless institution—its underlying mindset—may be responsible for damaging us, for causing us great pain. Consider, for example, individual Jews who were persecuted and damaged by the "master race" mindset under the Third Reich; or individual blacks who have been persecuted and damaged in South Africa by the apartheid mindset; or individual Native Americans who have been persecuted and damaged by the Eurocentric mindset. Consider also the damage done by the mindset that sanctified interring thousands of innocent Japanese-Americans in prison camps for the duration of World War II, and the deep damage many of us have suffered at the hands of certain dogmatic religious organizations.

In such cases, we have the same need to acknowledge the damage done to us, to express our pain and anger, and to ultimately let go, but we do not have a tangible figure—a familiar face and a personal history of one-to-one relationship—to address. Talking to abstractions—institutions or generalized mindsets—just doesn't do much for us. However, just as we enlist "Uncle Sam" to symbolize our otherwise faceless, soulless government, we can also enlist a familiar face to represent or symbolize any other institution we need to bring down (up!) to the human level. The following letter, for example, was directed toward Pope John Paul II, a figurehead of the entire institution of the Catholic Church or, more precisely, of the entire body of the doctrines (the mindset) of the Catholic Church.

> Dear Pope John Paul II,
>
> I am writing to you as part of a process I have begun to purge myself of the anger, the raw rage, I have long felt toward the Catholic Church, and for which I have, until recently, not found a proper outlet. This rage derives from all the years of psychological and spiritual abuse the Church has inflicted on me, through its misanthropic, inhumane teachings, from the time I was much too innocent, much too trusting, to be my own best authority on what was good for me and what was not. I am writing not as a way of condemning or punishing, but as a way of making peace with the past, of letting go, so that I might finally know the kind of inner peace only the truly compassionate, truly forgiving can ever know.

Here are the ways I feel that you, the Church, have
abused and damaged me:

- You instilled in me a belief that I was born
  inherently "bad," perverse, that I was sinful by
  the very nature of my being. You filled me with
  guilt and self-loathing before I had a chance to
  recognize and to celebrate the awesome, wondrous,
  one-of-a-kind miracle that I truly am.

- You taught me to regard everything having to do
  with sex as inherently evil, as "dirty"—as alluring bait atop the trapdoor to The Abyss. Even so
  much as an "impure thought," a mere fantasy, you
  instructed me, whether invited or not, was a most
  grievous infraction. I cannot begin to count the
  number of eternal nights I lay forcibly awake, as
  a wholly-believing child, in terror that should I
  fall asleep I would surely awaken in hell, because
  once again I had allowed myself to be seduced by
  the demon cinematographers within.

- You fostered in me the conceit that anointed
  Catholics are morally superior to all other
  human beings on the face of the earth, past and
  present, that Catholics are the favored children
  of "the Father" simply on the basis of their
  being Catholic, that all others, Protestants
  especially, are fallen and weak, creatures to be
  pitied. From your elevated pulpit of implied
  infallibility, you taught me chauvinism and
  elitism, rather than tolerance and acceptance.

- You closed my eyes, my heart, and my mind to all
  other possible paths to spiritual fulfillment.
  You put me in a room with no windows and shut the
  door. You taught me that there is only one true
  path, that all other paths are but the snares and
  traps of "false gods," that there is only one
  truth and one official oracle of this truth. You
  forced the tender feet of my soul into shoes into
  which they did not fit.

- You instilled in me the unacknowledged but deeply institutionalized notion that women are morally inferior to men, that women are unworthy even of meriting full citizenship in the circle of the truly chosen. You taught me to loathe and deny the essential feminine within myself.
- You robbed me of all hope of knowing perhaps the only joy that any of us can ever know, the kind that can only be realized in the paradise of the eternal moment. You taught me that I could know joy only through "redeeming" myself from my inherently fallen, inherently deficient, inherently perverted state of being, by punishing myself, by abasing myself, by flagellating myself. You taught me that if I wore a hair shirt of guilt and shame and self-denial long enough, if I suffered sufficiently, I would be rewarded in the end—after all chance of knowing joy in the moment, in the here and now, had been forever lost.

You taught me that spirituality is separation rather than connectedness, hierarchy rather than equality, judgment rather than compassion, guilt rather than joy, shame rather than self-esteem, blind faith rather than responsible mindfulness, pathology rather than sexuality, exclusion rather than acceptance, narrowness rather than richness, received truth rather than provisional truth, conquest rather than liberation, the way rather than a way.

You taught me that to believe in any way other than your way, to think in any way other than your way, to seek in any way other than your way, was to assign my soul to eternal damnation, to unrelenting torment. The truth, however, has been exactly the opposite. Your way has been a living hell for me on this earth and has brought me to the brink of spiritual annihilation.

But I forgive you. It wasn't your fault. Like all bureaucratic institutions, all human-wrought systems, the Catholic Church has, over the past 20 centuries, gradually, perhaps inevitably, evolved away from its original purpose, its founding principles. It has taken on a life of its own and has become almost wholly self-absorbed with its own perpetuation. I suspect that if Jesus—whose "Good News" was that the Kingdom of God is not in the hereafter, as Paul and Augustine and those other consummate misanthropes wanted us to believe, but in the here and now, within us, readily accessible to all who love unconditional-ly—if Jesus were alive today, he would feel more than a little ill-at-ease with a church that professes to be the embodiment of his own unconditional love but which teaches the exact opposite.

My hope is that one day you will come to see your role not as the fierce guardian of the one true path to spiritual fulfillment, but as the celebrant of all the paths; not as a spiritual monarch who must pretend to infallibility and perfection as the source of his absolute authority, but as a fellow traveler who shares equally in the common struggle, not as a judgmental parent who controls and manipu-lates young and vulnerable minds through fear and intimidation, but as a true spiritual father who loves all, accepts all, and embraces all—without condition.

Peace be with you.

(No reply to this letter was ever received. Some kind of acknowledgment would have been helpful, as all nods of the head by one human being to another are, but none was necessary.)

Getting to forgiveness is one of those concepts that sounds a lot easi-er in theory than it turns out to be in practice, especially when the amount of harm involved is more than significant. Indeed, the harm done to us by others can be like a gale blowing directly into our face, varying in strength with the depth and degree of the harm done.

Sometimes this gale can be overwhelming, even to the point of pushing us backward a bit, until we can regain our foothold; however, it is never insurmountable—never our master—unless, of course, we allow it to be.

Genesis

Before the beginning was the One, the Unknowable. In the beginning, the One divided itself into pairs mutually defining, mutually complementing, mutually opposing. First amongst these was Yin and Yang, Mother Spirit and Father Spirit, who created their children of themselves. The Mother breathed into her children the knowledge of life—rockeds, rooteds, leggeds alike; the Father breathed into them the knowledge of death.

When the kindred generations had grown into awareness, the Mother and the Father spoke to their children through the voice that whispers from leafy boughs within, "You are of the Mother and therefore mother with the Mother. You are of the Father and therefore father with the Father. You are life and you are death. Our gift to you is that you might know joy, but only through knowledge of its opposite. Our only commandment to you is that you strive . . .

To create Beauty
To be Beauty

To discover Truth
To be Truth

To attain Harmony
To be Harmony

To build Wholeness
To be Wholeness

Do these things and at the moment of your death the sweet essence of your soul will become as a smile on the face of all the waters of all the earth, for seven generations to come, for seventy times seven."

Making Peace With Ourselves

First keep the peace within yourself,
then you can also bring peace to others.
—Thomas á Kempis
Imitation of Christ
(c. 1420) Book II, Chapter 3

There is often great resistance to self-forgiveness, for like any signifi-
cant change, it is a death. It is dying to the habit of keeping ourselves
small and unworthy, dying to shame, guilt, and self-criticism.
—Robin Casarjian
Forgiveness: A Bold Choice for a Peaceful Heart

Nothing can bring you peace but yourself.
—Ralph Waldo Emerson
Essays: First Series

There is another side to forgiveness, as in the case of a large rock lying in a fallow field. The obvious side, the one fully exposed to our view, involves unresolved anger over the damage we have received. The less obvious side, the one facing the hard ground of our denial, involves unresolved guilt over the damage we have done.

Not only have we been betrayed and damaged, perhaps even grievously so; we, in turn, have betrayed and damaged others, perhaps even grievously so. This may be especially the case for those of us who are parents. To some very definite degree, though, it is—it has to be—true of all victims of personal or childhood trauma.

How could it be otherwise? As creatures of learned behavior, of mimic and modeling, we tend to do unto others as was done unto us—generation after generation. What we see, we do. What we hear, we say. What we receive, we give. What we are taught, we teach. What we inherit, we pass on. We do this until, perhaps reaching a crisis point, we turn over the rock that lays in our fallow field and allow ourselves to see the complete truth about ourselves—who we have become, what we have wrought. Enlightened by the truth, we can then empower ourselves to do whatever we must in order to break the cycle we have inadvertently become a part of.

The chronic anxiety we bear is a shifting kaleidoscope of angst that includes unresolved guilt over injuries inflicted in a past only selectively remembered. On some level, we all sense we have damaged or diminished others just as others have damaged or diminished us; that we have failed or betrayed the trust of others, just as others have failed or betrayed our own trust. Our unresolved guilt, blending with the more brilliant shades of our unresolved anger, distracts us. Its gravity pulls us ever deeper within ourselves. Its tyranny keeps us from plowing the fallow garden within.

Whereas unresolved anger, left unexpressed and unresolved, becomes hatred that poisons our soul, unresolved guilt, gone unexpressed and unresolved, becomes self-loathing that poisons our soul.

Guilt, like anger, is a natural defense mechanism, developed over eons of trial-and-error, "let's see what works" evolution. It serves the individual, and thereby the community at large, an essential service. It causes each of us to assess and control our behavior to the effect that we maintain a sufficient level of trust and respect in our relationships to prevent us from being alienated (banished) from the communities that are absolutely essential to our overall well-being.

In other words, guilt helps regulate our behavior. It pressures us to expend the precious energy necessary to change future behavior and to make just restitution for past behavior. If we fail to acknowledge and resolve guilt in the intended manner, we risk allowing it to ferment and be transformed, like sweet cider into acid vinegar, into a corrosive self-loathing that can eat away our tender soul. It is not enough, therefore, for us only to resolve our anger. If we are truly to let go and get on with it, we must also resolve our guilt. We must seek forgiveness from those we have damaged.

In reality, we may never actually achieve forgiveness from those we have damaged. Such forgiveness is not, and can never be, within our control. However, if we will earnestly seek it and make earnest efforts toward just restitution, we will eventually achieve permission to forgive ourselves.

Making peace with ourselves is a requires that we do the following:

- Acknowledge the damage we have done.

- Apologize for the damage we have done.

Acknowledging the Damage Done

Just as we had to fully acknowledge all the damage done *to* us, we must now fully acknowledge all the damage done *by* us. We must now take full responsibility for all the things we have done (or have failed to do) that have had a harmful, perhaps even traumatizing impact on others.

To do this, however, we may need to break through what may be the most impenetrable wall humankind is capable of building. Indeed, when it comes to protecting from the light of acknowledgment the truth about the harm we do, the walls of denial we build around this truth tend to take on the proportions of those massive mountains of stone that once protected medieval treasure rooms from all possible thieves.

In other words, for many of us, getting ourselves to acknowledge the damage we've done to others is likely to involve a lot more than simply bowing our heads under the full weight of an awful truth and acknowledging our culpability in a low, mournful voice. Not only must we chip, scratch, or claw our way through a wall of denial that may make the Great Wall of China look like a mere mound of flaccid sand bags, we must first acknowledge that such a wall even exists—camouflaged perhaps behind a manicured hedgerow of perky privets.

At this stage in his own journey, the author was faced with having to acknowledge the "impossible" truth that he had been physically and emotionally abusive toward his eldest son Joshua. He had to admit he had done his son a great deal of harm throughout his son's most formative years, the ones so crucial to developing life-launching and -sustaining levels of self-esteem and self-confidence. The choice was clear, but anything but simple: Either find the courage to own up to the terrible truth about himself and what he had done or build his wall of denial a little higher, a little thicker, and allow a young mind, a young heart, a young soul, sink ever deeper into the sucking mud of a swamp that, of course, was "not really there, because it couldn't possibly be."

By this time, after some sixteen years of imperceptibly incremental, consummately skillful stone-masonry, the author had all but completely walled the truth away from eyes he had in so many other ways developed into those of an eagle. In fact, a mere suggestion from his wife one evening that he was being abusive toward Joshua sent him into a rage of indignation and woundedness so consummately righteous that he felt compelled to threaten to "walk" if she were ever to make such an outrageous, humiliating suggestion ever again. (Oh, what power, that of the coward.)

In that moment, the author had so completely constructed his own private, comfortable reality, he truly perceived himself as a genuinely aggrieved party. One of the world's greatest injustices had just been committed against *him*—and by his own wife no less, the one person in this world he believed he could trust without reservation and would never "betray" him. *He* was the one who was being abused, for chrissake, not their son. Joshua didn't even know what pain was. How could he. He hadn't been through everything his father had been through.

In that "powerful" moment, there was no force on earth that could have caused the author to acknowledge the truth. The impenetrability of denial can be, and is, for a great many of us, that great. In fact, in the author's case, acknowledgment only came after he had begun to sink into yet another deep depression and, sensing he no longer had the personal resources to crawl out on his own (and perhaps sensing something else as well), he sought outside help.

In beginning a long, painful process to get at the roots of an accelerating tendency toward self-destruction, he inadvertently but unavoidably began a long, painful process of chipping away at an "impenetrable" wall of denial. Ultimately, he came to realize he could only save himself by saving his relationship with his son. Acknowledgment had become a matter of life or death, for two people. The author chose life, and therefore pain. But this pain, he was later able to see, was the agony of birth, rather than the torment of what otherwise could only have ended in irredeemable regret.

How long does this process of painful awakening typically take? It's not possible to say exactly, because some processes, such as this one, are not linear and therefore are not subject to easy measurement or prediction. In the author's case, a total of three and a half years lapsed from the time he entered individual therapy, at the very bottom of his depression, until he was able to write the following letter of acknowledgment to his son Josh. During those three and a half years, instead of smashing through walls of denial in the fashion of a TV superhero, he slowly chipped away at them, more in the fashion of a slowly warming sun melting a great glacier.

He chipped away a little from this spot, then a little from that spot, until finally little holes began to appear in the wall and more and more light began to diminish the darkness within. Magically, as in the case of the fictional vampire of Transylvania, the monster that lay within this darkness shrank and shriveled to the degree healing light was allowed to fall upon it. When, finally, there was no more darkness, there was no more monster. Liberated from his demon fear, the author could now fully acknowledge and own up to the entire range and depth of the harm he had done, not as a monster, but as a vulnerable, imperfect, reparably damaged human being.

One of the most exhilarating moments the author has ever experienced was the moment he dropped the following letter into a nondescript mail box:

> March 5, 1989
>
> Josh,
> I need to write this letter to you as one more stepping stone in my quest for spiritual health. I need to say this as a way of letting go, of moving on. Here goes:
> When you were a child, I was abusive toward you, both physically and emotionally. I caused you a great deal of pain. Perhaps worse, I caused you despair. I denied this in myself for many years; though a seeker of truth, I refused to see this truth. Even after I broke your wrist I would not see

it. I now know I was too blinded by misdirected
rage, by pride, by fear, to see it—too poisoned by
the past.

So powerful was my denial, in fact, so ugly, that
I once more or less told your mother that if she
ever again suggested that I was abusive toward you I
would leave her. Incredible, huh—but very real.

You have forgiven me, I know, and for this I am
profoundly grateful. And I want you to know that it
is a measure of your own inner strength and depth of
courage that you have turned out the fine young man
that you have. I am so very proud of you.

My hope for you now is that if you should choose
to become a father one day yourself, that you will
write the fatherhood scripts you will want to follow
well in advance, and that you will make them very
different from the ones I originally followed, from
the ones my father followed before me. It is in your
power now to break the cycle—for all time.

Thank you for hanging in there with me—and for
hanging in there for yourself.

Love. . . .

Sometimes, though, once is not enough. In fact, when it comes to fully
acknowledging the harm we do, once is probably *never* enough—for
either the acknowledgor or the acknowledgee. Indeed, the more often
we confirm the truth, the "truer," the more powerful, the truth becomes,
for all concerned.

The author wrote the following letter to his son Josh three years after
sending him the letter (above) in which the author initially acknowledged the harm he had inflicted on his son. The occasion was a crisis the
author had long been expecting. Josh was sinking into a depression root-
ed, the author sensed, in a chronic, debilitating lack of self-esteem.

March 30, 1992

Josh,
There are some messages for you in the enclosed
pages; see if you can find them. (The "enclosed

pages" consisted of the first few chapters of this book.)

Here is another message; see if you can accept it: Your problems with self-esteem do not stem from the abuse you suffered from school mates on the playground or at the bus stop. The damage had been done long before these unfortunate but relatively run-of-the-mill experiences. Your problems with self-esteem stem from the fact that your father was able to love you only conditionally during the most critical years of your life—not because you deserved to be loved only conditionally, but because I was too damaged during that time in the confluence of our lives to be able to do anything else.

No matter how much you may try to circumnavigate it, the inescapable truth remains: conditional love, especially in the extreme, is the most devastating force that can ever inflict potentially irreversible harm on the human spirit. And no matter how much admiration and respect and love you have for me now, no matter how much you might honor the special relationship you and I have now, you must face the truth of this fact.

You must face the absolute truth of the fact that that fateful October 1st in 1978 when I broke your wrist with my size-15 foot was not the only time I physically abused you, and that the number of times I punished you for not being perfect by withholding my love from you, by making you feel unacceptable, unlovable, were too numerous to even begin to recount. You must confront it, you must wrestle it to the floor, you must kick the livin' shit out of it. Nothing essential in your life will change, nothing will ever make it any better on the most fundamental levels of your being, until you do so.

Period.

Your crisis has come sooner than I thought it would, but I am glad. No pain, no gain—but the sooner one gets started on the real work, the less over-

```
all pain for the same gain. So, get yourself into
therapy, and if at any point you need me to attend
one of your sessions (something I highly recom-
mend), I'll be on the next plane. No, I cannot
make up for all the damage I did, I cannot make
things as they might otherwise have been, but I
can help you grow beyond the damage, perhaps even
well beyond it. And if I were to accomplish noth-
ing else in this life, that alone would be enough.
Absolutely.
     Time to get on with it.
     Love. . . .
```

As a result of this second letter, and the author subsequently threatening to call his son every hour on the hour until he made an initial
appointment to see a therapist (sometimes victims of depression need
a hefty amount of outside intervention; *believe it*), the author's son
eventually entered individual therapy. Within weeks, Joshua's depression had lifed (been let go of) and a true transformation had clearly
begun. (It took several years, however, for Josh to complete the slow,
painful process he had begun by entering therapy and thereby taking
responsibility for his life, for what his life was or was not to become.
Real change is *never* easy.)

In confronting and fully acknowledging the damage we have inflicted on others, we cannot escape experiencing some measure of pain.
This pain is much more likely to be the agony that accompanies birth,
however, than it is the eternal torment that accompanies irretrievable
loss or irredeemable regret. To bring this point "home," consider the
pain you would likely suffer, in a moment made eternal by its intensity, if you were to wait until the inevitable moment of your death to fully
acknowledge the extent of your failures and betrayals toward innocent
others.

If this thought alarms you, here are a few guidelines you may wish
to follow as part of your own process toward fully acknowledging any
harm you may have inflicted on others:

• **Serve an eviction notice on your demon fear.**
　　Of all the "demons" we harbor within, perhaps none is more
powerful, more controlling of us, than our demon fear. Indeed, as

long as we allow fear to sit on the throne of our personal sovereignty, we are not likely to find the courage to face up to all the things in our past we may need to face up to in order to be able to get on with it.

Am I fear-bound? Are most of my decisions fear-based? Would I be able to admit it to myself if I were fear-bound? These are the kinds of questions we must all face, head on, if we are to truly rule over our own personal sovereignty—if we are to ultimately find the courage to face the full truth about ourselves.

- **If you are not already in therapy, this might be an opportune time to start.**

Sometimes raw courage and good intentions need a helping hand. A *skillful* psychotherapist can be one such hand, by helping us chip away at whatever walls of denial we need to get past in order to get at the truth about ourselves. In particular, she or he can help us serve notice on our demon fear and depose the dirty old druid bodily from its claimed throne. Also, by reframing all those terrible, unforgivable "sins" we have committed, a skillful therapist can transform all those failures and betrayals into opportunities not only for redeeming ourselves but for moving our whole self to heights we might not otherwise have attained.

If nothing else, by serving as our unconditional advocate and cheerleader, a skillful therapist can help us extricate ourselves from a downward spiral of self-blame and self-pity. Until and unless we do this, we can do little else.

The key word is "skillful." Unfortunately, many psychotherapists today lack the proper training, skills, attitude, and/or temperament to be what we need them to be, that is, deserving of our absolute trust. In light of this unfortunate reality, you may wish to refer to Appendix C, "Choosing a Therapist," for a list of guidelines intended to help you protect yourself by finding not only a reputable therapist but the one who is right for you.

- **Take a "New Year's inventory" of any harm you may have inflicted on others.**

On the glare of a clean, white pad, write down all those moments in your life you would give almost anything to take back, especially the ones you've been working so hard to keep cowering well back in the shadows of your memory.

In addition, write down all those moments that, when viewed in isolation, do not appear to be all that harmful, but that take on a very different character when viewed in the aggregate or as a pattern. It is these latter moments that are often the most harmful of all.

For example, in making your list you may think of a time when you criticized your daughter for being too fat or your son for being too lazy. Perhaps there was "a scene." By itself, this incident may seem insignificant and not worth recording, much less remembering. ("Let sleeping dogs lie.") Subsequently, however, you remember and record other times when you made the same or similar criticisms (which may or may not have led to "a scene"). Over time, a pattern of criticism emerges from your list and you ultimately make a terrible connection: The criticisms you have directed at your daughter or son have severely eroded her or his self-esteem. They may even have all but destroyed it (perhaps to the point of precipitating an eating disorder or causing her or him to "drop out"). **Note:** If something like this happens to you, hang in there. All is not lost, unless you decide it is.

Be sure to write all these moments down, however much pain they evoke, as opposed to merely thinking about them in the elusive abstract. There is truly something magical about giving external body and voice to unpleasant, perhaps painful internal truths—precipitating a noxious haze into a liquid form we can then drain away. Indeed, the very act of writing or taping these truths—summoning the courage to do it—wrests their power away from them and hands it over to us. Thus empowered, we can begin to deal with these truths on our terms, to fully purge ourselves of their toxicity, as true masters of our own fate.

In this age of perceived powerlessness, it is easy for us to overlook just how powerful we truly are.

• **Avoid fatalistic "all or nothing" or "it's too late" thinking.**

Once we allow ourselves to think in terms of "it's too late, the damage has been done" or "if I can't make it all right, what's the use," it's over for us: We condemn ourselves to being forever stuck in the swamp of our eternal sorrows, and we fate all that we might have accomplished, all that we might have contributed, to being forever lost. From this moment on, therefore, instead of viewing yourself as a Johnny Come Too-Lately, you may wish to start viewing yourself as a Johnny Appleseed. Instead of completely surrendering your interior landscape to the tyranny of the briars and the nettles already growing there, you're going to start poking holes in the barren spots of your soul and dropping in seeds—one hole, and one seed at a time.

Indeed, over time, especially over the next several weeks and months, you're going to be planting a lot of seeds. Some of these seeds will sprout and grow and some will not, as it is with all seeds and all gardens. In the end, though, the overall landscape is going to be a lot better off for what you have contributed. It will not, however, be perfect. There may still be a few annoying nettles and a few barren spots, and some of the trees we plant may not bear much fruit. Even if it were perfect, though, by *whose* standards would we judge it so?

Fully acknowledging the damage we have done to others, including any damage we may have done to our own children, is a matter of making the truth tangibly real and therefore no longer deniable. We do this by putting our failures and betrayals toward others into words. We do it by recognizing and accepting that just as we were loved only conditionally (or not at all), we have, in turn, loved others only conditionally. What we inherited we have passed along in some form; what was done unto us we have done in some form.

We have an opportunity to break this cycle for all time. We also have the power. We can now begin a healing process that will affect not only all those to whom we have passed on our toxic legacy, but also all those yet to be touched by it—the "seven generations" to come.

Actually, we have already begun this healing process, by fully acknowledging the damage we have done. It is time now to apologize for it, and to offer to make amends.

Apologizing for Our Transgressions

Authentic apologies have become increasingly rare in this increasingly alienated and cynicized society we have both inherited and helped make. One reason for this is that when we injure people we don't have an intimate relationship with, we tend not to be concerned about them and their feelings as much as we would if we did have such a relationship. We don't "love" them, and we'll never see them again, so why trouble ourselves making apologies over trifles? Besides, who among them would apologize to us?

Another reason is that to apologize is to be prepared to bear the full cost of the consequences of our behavior. The trouble here concerns what "full cost" means in a society that has more lawyers than school teachers. If we were to be so foolish as to admit fault or blame for our mistakes, we fear, we'd end up being taken advantage of—"sued" in one form or another—to the fullest extent possible. In biblical terms, we'd be beaten and robbed and left bleeding by the side of the road.

In other words, people who don't deserve our trust don't deserve our apology.

What is being overlooked in this cynical attitude, born of mutual alienation and mistrust, is the magical, transforming power that the heart-felt, freely-given apology has on every soul it touches. Indeed, not only do the words "I'm sorry" have the power to transform both the apologor and the apologee, they can also transform any cynical bystanders that might be in the area of ground zero.

Although many of us are inclined to scoff at notions of alchemy and magical transformation, each of us has the power to effect just such a transformation: We can transform toxic "lead" into glittering "gold" simply by applying the elixir of a heart-felt apology to the festering wounds of a damaged relationship.

Only two things are required of us: (1) that we form our apology without condition or reservation, and (2) that we muster the courage to actually deliver it to the aggrieved party. In other words, we must be willing to make whatever amends are just and appropriate, and we must be able to overcome any fears:

- That our apology (and therefore we) will be rejected

- That those to whom we offer our apology will use our vulnerability to lash out at us

- That those to whom we offer to make amends will attempt to take advantage of us, by making unreasonable or even impossible demands

Considering the early experiences that forged us, such fears are likely to be very real, and overcoming them is likely to be no simple matter. Many of us have spent a lifetime avoiding making ourselves vulnerable to others in any way. We have learned that humans are generally not to be trusted (better to have a dog or a cat as a companion), that people's reactions can be terrifyingly out of proportion to the event triggering them, and that it is always less painful to view ourselves as less than courageous than it is to risk another perceived failure.

To get past this potential roadblock, we must come to accept that each of us already has within us all the courage we'll ever need to surmount whatever wall of fear may lay in our path. If at the moment we happen not to be in touch with this boundless reservoir for some understandable reason, all we need do is simply give ourselves time enough to do so. We'll get there. There is no more need for us to rush to transformation than there is for us to rush to wisdom or to maturity. We can move toward it as cautiously as we need to, as our particular circumstances warrant.

We may find that we need to focus our energy and courage on a single apology at a time. Or we may need to let our apologies sit in a drawer for a while. We may even need to move on to something else for some indefinite period of time. Our only obligation is that we keep our eyes fixed on where it is we eventually need to go. It is entirely up to us how we get there and how quickly we get there.

When the time comes for you to move toward apologizing for the harm you have done others, the following suggestions may help you along your chosen path:

- **Write or tape letters of apology for all those moments in your life that you would like to take back.**
  Fully acknowledge all the damage you have done—big and small. Be as complete and forthcoming as possible; however, in doing this avoid taking control of whatever list of wrongs you come up with: that is, be sure to leave the door open for the person you are addressing to acknowledge even more damage, or perhaps different damage. In other words, make your list of wrongs a working list rather than a final list—*the* list rather than *your* list. In fact, you may wish to explicitly invite the person you are addressing to present his or her perception of the damage you have done to them.

Also acknowledge the pain you may have caused the person you have injured, and apologize for it.

Don't hedge. Let go of any tendency to protect yourself by withholding or by couching.

• **Offer to make amends (and be prepared to make them).**

No mortal can pretend at being God and make everything be as it would otherwise have been. For us, Humpty Dumpty has fallen and not even all the "king's men" can restore what was, or effect what might have been. This kind of restoration, however, is not our goal. Our goal, a more modest one, is simply to restore a damaged or poisoned relationship to the extent we can once again, or perhaps for the first time ever, become a positive, supportive, nurturing force in this relationship.

Achieving this goal, however, requires something more than merely delivering the words—the surface—of an apology. It also requires that we prove the sincerity of our apology—to ourselves as well as to the aggrieved party. Not only must we offer to make just amends, we must also be prepared to actually make these amends, at whatever personal sacrifice is warranted.

A few cautions: In offering to make amends, avoid any tendency to define unilaterally (defensively?) what form these amends should take. Instead, be prepared to listen to and consider whatever amends the aggrieved party might request (or *demand*). Keep in mind there is at least some likelihood the aggrieved party will test you, by being at least modestly outrageous in his or her demands. Be patient. Listen to anything that is requested of you. If necessary, bite your lip, your tongue, whatever you have to. Ask yourself what *you* would be demanding if the shoe were on the other foot. Keep listening, keep talking. In time, the storm will blow itself out and whatever is both possible and reasonable will rise to a calm surface.

Also, resist any temptation to buy your way to atonement. For example, avoid trying to grant "just compensation" with gifts of a material nature. (These would really be for you, not for the aggrieved party.) If you offer to pay for psychotherapy for the aggrieved party, make sure you offer to participate in this therapy, in any way the aggrieved party might feel appropriate. The easy way out is no way out.

- **Avoid making any excuses or indulging in any self-serving self-pity.**

It can certainly be beneficial to mention in the context of your acknowledgments and apology the possible role family legacy has played in your behavior. The logic of cause and effect can be liberating for all concerned. However, you should be extremely careful not to do this as a way of deflecting blame away from yourself. ("The devil made me do it.") If the aggrieved party detects even the slightest attempt on your part to take less than full responsibility for everything that has happened—or if she senses you are attempting to use verbal tears and breast-beating as a way of winning her pity or deflecting her anger—you are likely to do more far more damage than good.

Your mission is to acknowledge the damage you have done, to take full responsibility for it, to apologize, and to offer to make just amends to the extent possible. In other words, your purpose is to give a precious gift *of self* to someone without any reservations, caveats, or hidden agendas.

- **Write several drafts of each letter you write or tape.**

You will likely need to generate several drafts of your letters (preferably over some unhurried period of time) in order to make them free of even the slightest hint of hesitation, hedge, fear, or personal agenda. To help you in this process, you may wish to have someone you trust read or listen to your letters. This person should be someone (a neutral party) who can place themselves in the shoes of your intended audience and see through their eyes. A therapist might serve this function.

Take your time because there's a lot at stake here. Harnessing all the horses of your courage to the carriage of your good intentions is not something you should rush. You don't want to end up with everything coming undone just as you're getting up to full speed.

- **Avoid attempting to control or manipulate the outcome.**

This is an especially tough one for "control freaks," those of us who believe that the only way we can be truly safe in this world is by controlling all things and all outcomes. If we are in *complete* control—if we play God—nothing can hurt us.

Unfortunately, there are two traps awaiting anyone who trods the alluring ground of this lovely logic.

1. There is precious little in this world we can truly control, including if not especially the reaction of those to whom we make apologizes and offers of atonement.

2. Attempting to control everything is ultimately and inevitably exhausting. Playing God cannot other than eventually deplete our stores of precious energy.

We can control the completeness and authenticity of the apologies we choose to make. We can even control whether or not we actually deliver these apologies. We cannot, however, do any more than this. We are not gods after all. Nor are we little merlins. We cannot control the thoughts and feelings of others, nor can we snap our fingers and make everything all right again.

What we can do is make an earnest and courageous effort toward restoring a damaged or poisoned relationship. If we will do this, we will move ourselves toward greening our garden within, and we will help another soul move toward greening his or hers. We will move closer to realizing perhaps the only paradise any of us can ever know.

On second thought, maybe we are gods after all.

• **Deliver your letters only when you are ready.**

After writing or taping your messages of acknowledgment and apology, you may sense a hesitation over actually delivering them. You're not ready, not yet comfortable. As the pilot of your own ship, you should not feel compelled to be ready, or in any way diminished because you are not ready. If you are not ready—if your season for planting the seeds of reconciliation has not yet arrived—then this is your truth and you should feel free to follow it. We are all the keepers of our own truth. If we are patient, our season always comes, just as surely as spring eventually emerges from winter—always on its own schedule, rather than in strict accordance with what the calendar might say.

Keep in mind that all this is a process. Sometimes it will go well and sometimes it won't. As previously suggested, one time it may not go well is when the aggrieved party receives your apology. Human nature being what it is, the person to whom you are apologizing may react to your apology by testing you in some way.

Again, you cannot control this. The only thing you can control is how you react to such a test. For example, you can allow yourself to get sucked into a shouting match, or you can bite your tongue and take whatever lashing the aggrieved party needs to give you as a way of testing you (and perhaps punishing you as well). The only way you can "win" in a situation such as this is to take the highest ground you possibly can and hang on as if for dear life.

In other words, if the aggrieved party needs to yell at you, let her yell; turn the other ear! Remember that once the aggrieved party sees she cannot provoke you into assuming your old ways, she will begin to believe in the magic of transformation. *(See also the chapter on rewriting our old scripts.)*

Because we live in a culture largely informed by male fears and notions ("Winning is not *every* thing; it's the *only* thing"), many of us construe apologizing with weakness and/or humiliation. The truth, of course, is that it takes far more strength and courage to apologize for wrongs done than it does to avoid facing up to them. We are far more likely to humiliate ourselves—in our own eyes especially—by failing to deliver an apology for lack of the raw guts to do so than we ever are by kneeling penitently before someone we have failed or wronged.

Some of us try to rationalize away this truth with some form of convoluted logic: *we're the real victim...that's not the way I remember it...it was their own damn fault.* When we try to clothe our cowardice in attitudes of Orwellian "double think," however, we fool ourselves but not the fate we are making for ourselves.

Apologizing is one of those "small" acts that—like making love—is both impossibly difficult and incredibly simple. It becomes impossibly difficult when we allow ourselves to be controlled by our fear-driven ego self. It becomes as easy as flipping a light switch when we listen to our courage-driven spiritual self.

Forgiving Ourselves

Even though it represents a large step in the right direction, seeking forgiveness from others—acknowledging the harm we have done and apologizing for it—is not enough. Even receiving the forgiveness we seek—should it actually be granted us—is not enough. In order for there to be any real change within us, we must also forgive ourselves—

not only for all the times we have failed or betrayed others, but also for all the times we have failed or betrayed ourselves.

We must forgive ourselves for all the times we've been neglectful or abusive, for all the times we've been stubborn or pigheaded, for all the times we've been weak or less than courageous, for all the times we've been unseeing or less than insightful, for all the times we've been self-centered or self-pitying, for all the times we've been bumbling or inept, for all the times we've been exploitive or manipulative. We must forgive ourselves for all the times we've been a complete and utter jerk.

We must forgive ourselves for the entire litany of the wrongs, injuries, failures, betrayals, stupidities, ineptitudes, wrong decisions, and lost opportunities we have accumulated over the span of our troubled tenure on this troubled planet. If we do not forgive ourselves—if we allow ourselves to be satisfied with the apologies we make to those we have wronged—we will be choosing to leave one leg still stuck in the sucking swamp of our guilt.

Normally, we would be able to see this—sense it. However, we may be too caught up in a giddy celebration over successfully extricating our other leg from the swamp to be able to do so. Or we may suffer from myopia in regard to selective aspects of our reality. Indeed, how many of us in looking at something unpleasant have not been able to adjust our focus to a comfortable blur?

The hard truth is that if we are ever to see ourselves as unconditionally lovable, truly so, we must forgive ourselves for all the harm we have done to others, as well as all the harm we have done to ourselves. To be truly free, we need to be able to feel—to believe—we are intrinsically deserving of the forgiveness and good will of others. Otherwise, whatever benefit we might derive from seeking the forgiveness simply will not last into the morning after our initial success. Inevitably, the leg we have freed will slip back into the swamp of our guilt.

At first glance, any attempt to forgive ourselves may seem like trying to clap in a concert hall with only one hand. How on earth can the transgressor forgive the transgressor? The wolf, the wolf? When we look a little deeper, however, we are reminded of a fundamental truth about ourselves: We are all of two distinct but inextricable natures, intermingled almost as if two separate beings were seamlessly blended into one. We have both a secular self (body mind) and a spiritual self (spirit mind). If we look still deeper, we are reminded that it is our secular self (the seat of our self-centeredness) that needs to be forgiven, and that it is our spiritual self (the seat of our unconditional compassion) that can—and will—do the forgiving.

Again, one size never fits all. Your process toward forgiving yourself has to be uniquely your own. However, you (both of you!) may find the following guidelines helpful:

- **Make a list of everything—the omissions, the failures, the betrayals—for which you need to forgive yourself.**

  The goal here is to capture the essence (not the fine details) of everything you have done or have failed to do in the past that tends to hang onto you, or you onto it, because of the sucking pull of the guilt or anguish it causes you—the diminishment in self-esteem it causes you. An exhaustive, absolutely comprehensive enumeration of all your "sins" is not required.

  For example, if you've spent the last ten years berating or punishing your children (with incessant criticism or worse) for not being everything you are not and will never be, write this down. If you've spent the last fifteen years blaming others for everything that is wrong in your life, instead of choosing to recognize and acknowledge your own role (subtle or otherwise) in all the failures and disappointments in your life, write this down. If you've spent the last twenty years looking after "numero uno," fortressing both self and possession against the inevitable betrayal and bad faith of others, write this down.

  Write down everything you think of, in the order in which it occurs. There is absolutely no need to make any judgments or edits.

- **In a mirror, look your ego self straight in the eye and verbally forgive her.**

  Say the words out loud: "I forgive you. I forgive you for all of it." Avoid simply saying the words internally or just thinking them in the abstract. Again, it is a much more powerful experience to fully embody a thought or truth by giving it real flesh and real voice, than it is simply to acknowledge its presence as it flashes fleetingly across the gray screen of your conscious mind. Consider the difference between simply scanning a sheet of flag-waving notations on a sheet of paper and listening to the same arcane abstractions embodied by a full symphony orchestra.

You may wish to forgive yourself individually for each one of the transgressions you have written down. As you do this, allow yourself to become aware of who is speaking, that is, where your "forgiveness voice" is coming from.

At first blush, this exercise may sound a little silly. For those of us who have had unpleasant role-playing experiences, it may remind us of the embarrassing artificiality and awkwardness we felt in those perhaps-coercive situations. However, once you have fully acknowledged the power and reality of your spiritual self—spirit mind—you are not likely to have any trouble "getting into" this exercise. In fact, don't be surprised if you shed a few tears you didn't realize were still trapped within you. If this exercise does not work, try the following alternative.

• **As an alternative to the above option, write yourself a letter.**
Write a letter to yourself (to your body mind) forgiving her for all her transgressions against you, just as you might write a letter to a parent (or anyone else) forgiving them for all their transgressions against you. In fact, you may wish to go as far as to actually send this letter to yourself and then read it out loud when you receive it.

Once we are in touch with it—fully empower ourselves with it—our spirit mind is capable of great "medicine." It is this part of ourselves that is the source of all the power and courage any of us will ever need to get us to where we truly need to go.

Pilot of Your Own Ship

Something awakens you from the tossing and turning of a restless sleep. Above the low hum of your miraculous brain, a voice more felt than heard, the kind easily lost in the relentless din of the life little questioned, is whispering to you from an unfathomable depth within. "It is time," it is saying. "You are ready now. Your hour has come."

Inky darkness engulfs you, but you are not afraid. There are no demons within, therefore there can be none without. A crystalline light appears above the foot of your bed, pulsating in easy respiration, like a flashing beacon marking safe passage along a rocky coast. Arising without hesitation, you follow this breathing light as you would your own truth, passing freely through a catacomb of narrow corridors and windowless rooms, each familiar yet foreign, until you find yourself standing before the imposing barrier of a heavy metallic door, its corners more rounded than square.

You have been here before. You ventured no further then, fearing what might lay in wait on the other side. But this time you feel no urge to turn and flee, to return to the comfortable familiar. You are ready. Your hour has arrived.

Grasping the door handle, cold to your touch, you are surprised by how easily this massive, seemingly immovable metal door yields to your will. You feel your face soften into a smile, for this is not the first time you have believed one thing only to discover quite the opposite to be true. As you swing the door fully open, the surrounding darkness gives way to the stinging glare of unfiltered light. Casting your eyes toward the metallic floor, which seems to be undulating ponderously beneath you, like some insidious carnival ride designed to disorient and intimidate, you allow your eyes time to adjust, just as they have been miraculously designed to do.

When finally you lift your eyes, you find yourself surrounded by a seamless arc of glass, looking out onto the infinite expanse of churning, windswept sea. Directly in front of you stands a large, spoke-handled wheel, lashed into stasis by a web of ropes, seemingly of various sizes and constituencies. To the right of the tethered wheel stands a brass compass, fastened atop a post like a parking meter.

Peering past the wheel, through the seamless window, you see—dead ahead!—a massive mountain of ice protruding from the sea like a great pyramid in a desert of undulating dunes. Though a chill passes down your spine, you do not feel your head go numb with fear. You do not turn your back and flee to the safety of the dark catacombs within. You know what you must do.
You are ready.

The stiff hemp is resistant to the urgent fumblings of your fingers, unfamiliar with the task at hand, but one by one the taut knots yield to your will, as inevitably they must. Finally the last knot is loosened and the helm becomes wholly free in your hands—alone. Gripping the spokes on the wheel firmly, you can feel the awesome power of the momentum that is carrying you forward, on a collision course with the massive shoal of ice dead ahead. But you are not afraid.

You are ready.

Lifting with one arm, pushing with the other, you attempt to torque the helm, to change the course of your destiny, but the accumulated momentum is too great; the rudder below will not budge against the great weight of the water rushing against it. Closing your eyes, you remember a dream in which an unseen demon is chasing you; your legs feel as if you are running knee-deep in thickening molasses. "It's too late," a familiar voice whispers in your ear. "Your destiny is sealed."

Filling your lungs with an unhurried breath, you visualize yourself moving toward a bright light on a darkening horizon, flowing as if riding the crest of an eternally curling wave. The bright light grows warm and soothing on your face, like a spring sun emerging from behind vanishing clouds. A profound sense of well-being begins to fill every crevice of your being.

Swelling your chest with another slow, deep breath, you summon from an unfathomable depth within the full presence of something that, until now, you have only sensed languishing there, and bring it to bear on the great wheel of your destiny. You feel the helm, the rudder below, begin to yield to your indomitable will. You feel the momentum of the great ship of your destiny begin to shift.
You are now pilot of your own ship.
You are ready.

Rewriting
the Old Scripts

When we grow up, many of the protective strategies (our former child self) developed tend to work against us. This is true of many effective and creative ways of surviving. Often, the very things that keep a child safe are the opposite of what an adult needs to have an effective, healthy life.
—Nancy J. Napier
Recreating Your Self

We all use scripts to automate our behavior in certain recurrent or familiar situations. We do this because Nature designed us to be as efficient as possible, for the sake of efficiency itself (the benefits that derive therefrom) and as a way of expediting behavior that can be critical to our survival. In effect, scripts automate our behavior to the effect that all we need do in a particular situation to trigger a (hopefully appropriate) response is simply press an invisible button, as opposed to having to deliberately sort through and weigh all the possible courses of action.

For example, imagine you confront a lean and hungry saber-toothed tiger one late afternoon while you're out gathering wildberries for breakfast. On the basis of similar encounters, you have written a script as a way of automating your reaction to first sight of this fearsome beast. You did this because you adjudged this animal to be much too dangerous to deal with in a conscious, deliberate manner, one that would invite possible error.

Instead of trying to reason out an appropriate response, you simply press an invisible button. Your script becomes your lord and master. Instead of sprinting toward the nearest tree, you obediently freeze in your tracks. You become as inanimate as that tree itself, and thereby completely invisible to an animal that, you have previously observed, reacts only to motion.

Your script has saved your life.

For many of us, however, these behavior-automating scripts, instead of protecting us from the fangs of the saber-toothed tigers in our lives, real or imagined, can often be counterproductive to our own best interests. They can sometimes even be injurious to us. In fact, many of our scripts, instead of putting our rational adult self in control in familiar or recurrent situations, place the wounded, desperate child we once were in control.

For example, the same "escalation" script we used as children to win petty arguments (we simply *had* to win, in order to protect from the shame of losing) may now tend to draw us into arguments in which we escalate our aggressiveness to the threshold of violence. The "gotta win no matter what" mentality reflected in this script is effectively keeping the needy child we once were firmly in control, instead of serving to keep the reins of control firmly in the hands of our mature adult self, where it belongs. The end result is likely to be ever greater degrees of alienation from the family members and peers with whom we argue. It is also likely to be ever deeper levels of self-loathing.

As with any tool, scripting our reactive behavior can be either a positive force in our lives or equally its opposite. The hammer can build up, the hammer can tear down. Scripting our behavior can empower us and serve our best interests; it can enslave us and serve no one's best interests. Which of these potentials is the case is, as with all matters of personal behavior, always a choice—one that, unlike an early-morning frost on a window pane, never goes away.

In this chapter, we will identify the old scripts that are currently enslaving rather than empowering us. We will then start rewriting these old scripts to put our adult self, rather than the desperate child we once were, firmly in control.

Ode to Joy

Rewriting counterproductive scripts is potentially one of the most liberating, empowering exercises those of us who have become enslaved by our old scripts can ever hope to undertake as willful, sentient creatures. Rewriting our scripts puts our adult self—our king or queen—firmly and fully in charge of our behavior and therefore our fate. Perhaps surprisingly, it is also provides us with the potential for a great deal of pure, unadulterated fun! Humor, after all, springs from the unexpected.

Consider the potential for some good fun in a situation in which your parent had previously always been able to draw you into a major argument, or lay a major guilt trip on you, every Christmas. Suddenly you're not playing by the old script anymore. No matter what your parent does to draw you into the same old routine, you're not budging. The more your parent tries to draw you in, the more he or she becomes a caricature of his or her own ferocity, Instead of an elephant hiding under the rug in the living room, there's now a clown performing in center ring. It certainly would not be advisable for you to laugh openly at the comical sight before you, but you may wish to have a few chuckles in the privacy of your own well-deserved self-satisfaction.

Consider also the comical confusion of the child who makes the same old "mistake" but does not get the same old reaction from you. Instead of criticizing and shaming, belittling and diminishing, you simply smile. And only you know why.

Indeed, there is much amusement to be had at the expense of those in our lives whom we send scrambling to adjust to the new self we show in old situations.

At first glance, though, rescripting ourselves to address a seemingly infinite number of situations can seem a daunting, perhaps even overwhelming, task, especially if we allow ourselves to assess it in the whole—as when we make the mistake of viewing from the very bottom the summit of a mountain we are being asked to climb. In the extreme, we might perceive rescripting ourselves as being tantamount to wholly remaking ourselves.

If, however, we are able to keep our attention focused on only one small step and hand-hold at a time, we will soon discover that the most difficult part of rescripting ourselves, as in getting a flow of water started, is getting the process primed—putting in place the first new script.

Thereafter, propelled by growing feelings of liberation and empower-ment, we will find each new script increasingly easier to write and implement, until ultimately we find ourselves plugging them into our *modus operandi* for the pure joy of it.

Who's in Charge?

Just for the fun of it, place yourself in each of the following situa-tions:

1. While you are commuting to work through the usual heavy traffic, the driver of a car in the adjoining lane suddenly pulls directly in front of you, in your lane, without first sig-naling his intentions.

2. While reaching across the table for something she should have asked to be passed to her, your nine-year-old daughter spills her milk . . . all over the table . . . all over the floor . . . all over your lap.

3. A telemarketer calls you on the phone during your favorite TV program and asks you to sponsor a handicapped child to the Bozo Brothers Circus.

4. You are overwrought with chores at home and duties else-where and neither your spouse nor your children seems to notice.

5. While visiting your parents over a holiday, your mother nags you about your weight, as usual.

6. While shopping at the local mall in mid-October, you find several of the shops already displaying Christmas decora-tions, some even playing Christmas music in the back-ground.

7. At a cocktail party, a man you just met makes a remark that you find offensive or that you strongly disagree with.

8. During dinner at home, your twelve-year-old son is conde-scending, almost mocking, in taking issue with something you feel strongly about.

9. Upon returning home from grocery shopping, you discover that you have forgotten to buy the key ingredient you need for dinner that evening.

10. Entering the kitchen after your children have finished eating their lunch, you notice they have not wiped down the table and counter tops to your standards.

11. Someone of lesser experience at work offers to take some of the load off your shoulders in order to help you meet a critical deadline.

12. You spouse asks you, "Where are you? You never tell me what you're thinking."

What is likely to be your reaction in each case? Is it likely to be a response that has been very deliberately weighed and measured by your conscious mind, the result of bringing to bear the full set of values and aspirations you hold within your true self? Or is it more likely to be a reflexive response, dictated by a script you (or someone else) has previously embedded deep within the holographic layers of your miraculous brain, to be triggered by familiar or recurrent situations?

Is your reaction likely to leave you feeling you have done the right thing, that you have made a positive contribution to your own life as well as to the lives of those directly affected your reactions? Or is the opposite more likely to be true?

If we are survivors of personal or childhood trauma, we are likely to conclude that a great deal of our reactive behavior is automated to work in negative ways. Some of it is even directed to work in destructive ways—not only grossly and visibly, but also subtly, almost invisibly.

Of course, there is a logic underlying this truth about us, and we would do well now to take a moment to gain a little insight into this logic. Insight brings understanding; understanding, forgiveness; forgiveness, empowerment.

The Need For Scripts

Human beings intrinsically have a hierarchy of needs, or interests, that relate directly to the survival and well-being of each individual and thereby to the community or species as a whole. The most basic of these interests is simple physical survival—getting enough to eat and staying out of harm's way. Unless this most basic need is assured, all else is moot.

Toward this end, Nature has endowed us with a variety of facilities to help us be responsible for our own survival. Among these facilities is the ability to perceive patterns of events, especially threatening events, and to generalize on the basis of these patterns. In addition, we have the ability to automate our response to these patterns in order to ensure both the most effective response and the quickest possible response. Under normal circumstances, these facilities work very well.

To pick up our earlier example, we might observe that the saber-toothed tiger only gives chase when we (or its other prey) moves. On the basis of this observation, we formulate a hypothesis: "If we remain still, instead of running for the nearest tree, we will be safe." We then write a simple script that automates our response to the merest sight of this dire threat: "Freeze!"

At the same time, we generalize both our hypothesis and our script in order to be as inclusive of all the possibilities as possible. We say to ourselves: "All fanged, snorting, meat-eating animals resembling the saber-toothed tiger may become a dire threat when we attempt to run away from them." We then apply our expanded hypothesis and script to every animal we encounter that resembles—even remotely—the saber-toothed tiger. We do this simply because it's always better to err on the side of conservatism—in other words, to be safe rather than sorry (dead).

As time goes by, the more animals we encounter that confirm our hypothesis, the more liberally we apply our script, and, unavoidably, the more unconscious of applying it we become. Under the right circumstances, we might reach the point where we no longer dare venture away from the camp to pick berries. Everything out there has become a "saber-toothed tiger."

When an individual is immersed in an environment in which she encounters contradictory patterns of behavior in the same object, or in which she encounters an entire reality that seems turned upside-down (pain is love, parent is child, trust is betrayal, anxiety is normal), what was meant to be a basic survival facility, or tool, can easily become distorted into its very opposite.

Consider the victim brought up in alcoholic home: Very early on, this individual observes that when Dad is drunk there is always conflict—another argument over absolutely nothing of consequence—and this conflict invariably escalates into violence. Dad beats up the victim, or he beats up Mom, and the next morning he utters profuse "swear to God" apologies and promises of change—all of which, of course, he soon breaks.

As a matter of basic survival, this victim formulates hypotheses on the basis of the patterns of Dad's threatening behavior, writes scripts to automate his responses to this behavior, and makes appropriate generalizations in order to be as inclusive as possible. In the end, this victim's scripts might be summed up as follows: "Avoid *all* conflict with Dad. Do not trust *anything* the son-of-a-bitch says."

In the context for which it is originally intended, this script serves the victim very well. By protecting the victim from getting into arguments with Dad, and from relying on Dad's promises concerning future conflict and violence, the behavior automated by this script protects the victim from being beaten up, perhaps even from being severely injured. Unfortunately, though, the victim's early hypotheses and generalizations concerning Dad's behavior are not likely to end with Dad. Over time, the victim is likely to generalize on the basis of her immediate experience to include more and more types of authority figures, as well as more and more instances of conflict and promise. Gradually, insidiously, the victim comes to view *all* authority figures as threats and traitors, *all* promises as falsehoods.

In other words, a generalized strategy that was once rational and beneficial—avoid all conflict with Dad, whether he's drunk or not; never trust any of Dad's promises—becomes increasingly irrational, and therefore increasingly counterproductive, as the scope of generalization widens beyond the source of the initial danger. The process only accelerates if the victim's fear is reinforced by injuries or betrayals suffered at the hands of other players, such as siblings, peers, teachers, lovers, or clerics.

In the extreme, the victim avoids not only every situation in which conflict is certain, but also every situation in which there is only the merest potential of conflict The victim also sees the demon face of betrayal in almost every spoken word, whatever its source. In other words, a script for survival becomes a script for ever deepening alienation and anxiety. Dr. Jekyll transfigurates into Mr. Hyde, never to return to his original self.

Taking a Second Look

What worked for us in the past—the beliefs, coping strategies, scripts—sometimes does not work for us in the present. As the context changed, we did not appropriately adjust our beliefs and thereby our coping strategies and our scripts. Now we have no choice: If we are to truly get on with it, we must make real changes, perhaps even major changes, to how we react to certain familiar or recurrent events. Before we can effect the changes we need to make, however, we must know exactly what it is we need to change. We must identify—and acknowledge—specifically what is not working. In other words, we must take a look at the full spectrum of our reactive behavior, at the old scripts that define this behavior, and make some kind of judgment about what is working in our favor and what is working to keep us mired in the swamp of our victimhood.

What we must do, then, in effect, is to become objective observers of ourselves. When we react to familiar or recurrent events—such as someone inviting us to participate in an activity for which we have had no previous experience—we must raise our conscious awareness to the point we take unabridged notice of our reactive behavior, almost as if we were having an "out-of-body-experience" dressed in a white lab coat, holding a clipboard. We must identify and fully acknowledge the role we play—the script we obediently follow—no matter how unseemly our behavior may appear to us from our out-of-body vantage point, and we must identify precisely what triggers our obedience to this script.

For example, we may observe that, in reaction to the invitation to participate in an activity for which we have had no previous experience (cross-country skiing, for instance), we come up with a clumsy excuse ("I can't; I have a bad knee") before we've even had a chance to consider the overall merits of the invitation. The trigger to this response may be a generalized fear of being scorned or laughed at for our chronic ineptitude or lack of "competitive acceptability." In other words, through conscious observation, we come to recognize that our reaction in this case—telling a lie— is that of the helpless, wounded child we once were. The trigger for telling this lie, we see, is a generalized fear—of being rejected—being harbored by this same child.

Notice that underlying the generalized fear of this child, and her resultant coping script, is a set of interrelated beliefs: I am incompetent...my incompetence will be scorned or laughed at (and deserves to be)...being laughed at is being rejected. Notice, too, that this interrelationship is highly recursive.

- In fearing rejection (being scorned, laughed at), our child tends to avoid any situation in which she is all-but-certain to demonstrate her ineptitude.

- In avoiding situations for which she has little or no previous experience, she denies herself the opportunity of gaining the experience she doesn't have.

- By denying herself the experience she doesn't have, she deepens her feelings of incompetence and ineptitude.

- By deepening her feelings of incompetence and ineptitude, she even further generalizes her fear of being scorned and rejected.

In other words, the legacies of our former child self, left unchallenged, tend to trap us ever deeper in recursive cycles that lead us ever deeper into the swamp of our victimhood.

Time to take charge? Time to get on with it?

The following suggestions may help you lift the burden of your adult life from the fear-driven, wounded child you once were.

- **Record your reactive behavior (scripts) in a journal.**
  As you become aware of the scripts that define your reactive behavior in familiar or recurrent situations, record the essence of these scripts in a private journal. Begin with a brief summary of the circumstances that led to your following a particular script: Place the event in a general category. ("I encounter an authority figure.) Then summarize details of the specific event. ("While out shopping at the mall during the noon hour today, I spotted my boss coming toward me but not yet seeing me.")

Concentrate on those circumstances and scripts that result in a negative outcome: shame, guilt, anger (at self, at others), alienation, fear, diminishment of self-respect, despair, whatever. Also record what seems to be the trigger for each script (fear, resentment, jealousy, etc.) and what the underlying beliefs seem to be. ("I am powerless in the presence of an authority figure; I am at risk of being harmed.")

The magic we are using here is the same magic we used in the previous chapter to help us fully acknowledge the damage that was done to us when we were children. By translating abstract notions and observations into concrete terms, we tend to make these notions and observations "more real." We also tend to stimulate our thinking about these notions and observations and give them more energy.

Note: It is not necessary for us to get it exactly right—to identify the precise trigger or the precise underlying beliefs. What's important is that we begin to become aware of our particular scripts, the circumstances under which these scripts are triggered, and why we may have come to write and follow these particular scripts. In other words, our goal is awareness—the source of all real self-empowerment.

• **Avoid any self-blaming over what you see.**
Remember hearing your own voice for the first time as others hear it, recorded on tape? Or seeing yourself for the first time as others see you, in a photograph or captured on film? Remember how surprised you were? How embarrassed? How apologetic? How self-deprecating, self-blaming, self-flagellating? As a result of what you experienced, did you actively seek to hear more of your "real" voice, or to see more of your "real" self?

Seeing your reactive behavior as an outside observer would see it may bring on similar responses and feelings, especially if you observe yourself having a particularly negative impact on others. Try to keep in mind that the behavior you are observing belongs not to you but to someone you once were—a wounded, desperate, needy child who did what was necessary to survive. You are now lifting from the shoulders of this former self the burden of conducting your adult life, so that your child self may finally rest in peace, and so that your adult self can finally get on with it.

- Return to the previous chapter and reread the suggestions for letting go of your "child within.'

As mentioned earlier, each step in the process of getting on with it is related—interwoven with—all the other steps, as is clearly evident at this point in our overall process: We see now that we cannot rescript ourselves without first, simultaneously, or eventually coming to terms with the author of the original scripts.

It may be helpful at this point to take a look at some example journal entries. Each of the following entries maps back to one of the items in the list at the beginning of this chapter.

Example 1:

Someone treats me unfairly (disrespectfully): On my way to work this morning, another driver suddenly swerved into my lane directly in front of me, obviously trying to beat me past the car that had been directly in front of him. The driver was talking on his car phone. I had to hit the brakes.

Script: I raged as if I had been personally violated. I laid on the horn—I swore a string of epitaphs—I gave the guy the bird. I was still pissed off when I got to work. I had a donut to make myself feel better, but, of course, that only made me feel worse. Thereafter, everybody I encountered seemed to be a jerk, out to "get" me. This one "little" incident ruined my whole day.

Trigger: Anger, resentment.

Underlying Beliefs: The world is full of rude, selfish, self-absorbed assholes who don't give a damn about anybody but themselves. No one is to be trusted to treat me fairly and respectfully. Expect the worst from everybody because that's exactly what I'm going to get. It's my sacred responsibility to make these people aware of just what idiots they are, and to punish them accordingly.

Example 2:

Someone "under my control" makes a mistake: Emily spilled her milk at the table again. As usual, she reached when she should have asked.

Script: I yelled at her—for reaching instead of asking, for not doing as she's been told over and over again. I slapped the offending hand, then made her go to her room. Dinner was ruined. Later, feeling guilty, like a jerk, I went to her room and apologized, selfishly seeking enough forgiveness so I could sleep.

Trigger: Fear.

Underlying Beliefs: I need to be perfect in order to be accepted and loved; therefore, everybody under my control (whom I view as an extension of my self) needs to be perfect. If I am not perfect—if the people under my control are not perfect—I will not be acceptable, either to myself or to anyone else.

One's children are an extension of one's self.

Example 3:

Someone makes a request of me: Another insincere solicitor called me during dinner today and asked me to sponsor a retarded child to some circus that was coming to town.

Script: Though I was angry to be solicited at home by phone, especially during the dinner hour, I stood there and listened to the entire pitch, while my dinner got cold, then I said "yes" when what I really wanted to say was "no"!

Trigger: Guilt.

Underlying Beliefs: If I do not help small, helpless persons onto whom I project my own woundedness, I will be racked with guilt.

If I say no to the requests people make of me (even people I do not even know!), their feelings will be hurt.

Again, it is not necessary for the analyses reflected in these entries to be exactly right—to identify the precise trigger or the precise underlying beliefs. If we are persistent and conscientious, if we simply "give it our best shot," the kind of self-awareness we are seeking will occur, over time, despite whatever imperfections we bring to the overall exercise. Think "process" rather than "result."

Before we move on to rewriting our old scripts, let's take a look one last example, this one dealing with Christmas ("family-orientated" holidays in general), a holiday that seems to be particularly troublesome for victims of family dysfunction:

> Christmas:
> **I feel obligated to make everybody else happy:**
> It's not even Thanksgiving yet and already I'm feeling the old anxieties about getting everybody the "right" gifts for Christmas—"right" being sufficiently appropriate and sufficiently large—and for making Christmas a happy occasion for everybody in general.
> **Script:** I shop until I drop. I read through all the catalogs. I bake cookies. I make and buy the decorations. I decorate the house. I send out all the Christmas cards. I give money to all the charities. I wrap all the gifts. I plan and cook a big Christmas Day dinner. I lead the caroling. I feel guilty for not having done enough.
> **Trigger:** Guilt.
> **Underlying Beliefs:** I am the responsible one. If I don't do it, nobody else will; the whole thing will be a disaster and it will be my fault.

It's time to take charge.

Taking Charge

When we rewrite the old scripts, we take charge; we take responsibility. We choose to be the adult self we were intended to be—to let go of the child self we no longer can afford to be. We liberate ourselves, we empower ourselves. We become the author of the masterpiece that our life was meant to be, and shall now become.

But taking charge is not intending it...is not planning it out in excruciating detail...is not playing it out in fantasy. Taking charge is doing it. Here are a few suggestions you may find useful.

- **Rewrite the beliefs underlying the old script.**

Our behavior—especially our reactive behavior—is largely a reflection of fundamental beliefs we hold about ourselves, about others, and about the world in which we live. To change our behavior, therefore, it is always more efficient (though not absolutely necessary) to change the old beliefs that underlie this behavior, or at least to apply a little pressure to these old beliefs, to see how well they stand up.

For example, those of us who avoid authority figures, or defer to them in a self-deprecating manner, may try to "get even" with them in the totally safe, absolutely controllable realm of fantasy or vicarious experience. We do this because we have come to believe that all authority figures are a threat and are therefore either to be wholly avoided or wholly appeased. The only place we can feel more powerful—safely dominant—is in fantasy, or through some kind of projection or identification, as when we become a fierce fan of a professional sports team.

To change our behavior, we have two choices:

1. We can consciously control our behavior each time we encounter, or anticipate encountering, an authority figure.

2. We can change what we believe about authority figures (in general) and simply allow ourselves to behave accordingly. Both approaches can "get the job done." The first approach however, is likely to require that we spend energy on being vigilant and consistent that we would not otherwise have to spend.

In the real world we cannot simply decide to supplant an old belief with a new one and instantly have the new belief expunge all traces and influences of the old one. We can, however, make ourselves aware of how irrational and counterproductive an old belief is, and we can consciously remind ourselves of just how appropriate and hopeful a new, rationally distilled belief is. We can then be patient with ourselves, with our inevitable inconsistencies, while we gradually, by fits and starts, internalize this new belief.

If it takes twenty-one days to supplant an old habit with a new one, can we expect anything less in supplanting an old belief?

Hint: Put in words, down on paper, each new belief (or set of beliefs) you intend to use to supplant an old belief, perhaps even side-by-side with the old belief. In fact, you may find it useful to divide into two columns each page of the loose-leaf notebook you will be using for recording all of your old, counterproductive scripts, so you can record the old behavior and the old underlying beliefs in one column, the new behavior and the new beliefs in the other (or you may wish to use facing pages). Also, you may wish to use lead pencil instead of ink, at least for recording the "new" entries, so you can readily make the edits and adjustments that, even if you are a veritable Shakespeare, you will find inevitable in your quest to author yourself into the masterpiece you were meant to be.

• **Rewrite the old script.**

What we choose to believe suggests how we wish to behave. For example, we might choose to believe (or to continue to believe) that all authority figures will take advantage of us in some way (physically, socially, mentally, educationally, economically, politically) should we give them the slightest opportunity. Our behavior toward these authority figures will flow from our chosen belief as heat from fire, as water from melting ice (we will avoid, defer, appease, grovel, fantasize); the one is simply another form of the other. Likewise if we choose to believe that no authority figure, no matter what his or her secular stature might be, has any real power over us, over our intrinsic worth as a fellow human being (we will look them in the eye, be ourselves, tell the truth as we know it, and stick up for ourselves).

Once again, we are reminded of the interconnectedness—the nonlinear interdependency—of all the individual "parts" of any process for getting on with it. We see that we cannot replace our old counterproductive behaviors with new productive ones without knowing what we believe. We also cannot determine what we believe without being in touch with who we really are— that is, with the values and needs that resonate with the deep cords of our true self. In other words, before we can prescribe behavior that will best serve not only ourselves but all whom we touch, we must first be fully aware of what kind of person we truly are, what it is we truly hold most dear, and what kind of legacy we truly wish to leave behind. (**Note:** We deal with these "first cause" issues in greater detail in the following chapters. Once again, because of the nonlinear interdependence that is evident here, you are encouraged to read through the entire guide book before taking any specific action relative to any specific issue. Context is everything!)

It may be helpful at this point to take a look at some example replacements of old counterproductive scripts—the scripted behavior and the beliefs underlying this behavior. Each of the following scripts corresponds to one of the example journal entries in the preceding section ("Taking a Second Look").

Example 1:
   Situation: A driver pulls in front of me without signaling.
   Category: Someone treats me unfairly or disrespectfully.
   New Beliefs: There are certainly plenty of rude, selfish, self-absorbed people in this world, and this person may well be one of them. But not all people are this way. In fact, it is probably true that the majority of my fellow travelers on this earth are generally of good will; the meek of spirit are simply less visible. It is not my job to judge and punish others, but, instead, to serve as a model of what I expect of others, what I hope for in them; I will not influence everybody in this way; however, if I am consistent, I will make a difference. No one can make me cynical; only I can inflict the corrosive rot of cynicism on myself.
   New Script: I will take a slow, deep breath and consciously remind myself that this person's behavior is not everybody's behavior, that it was not deliberately aimed at me, that its impact on me and my life is microscopically

small. I will flash my lights, once, just to let
this person know that I am a person too, deserving of his consideration and respect; I will
not, however, attempt to punish him or retaliate
with any outpourings of venomous words and gestures. I will let go.

I will congratulate myself for staying in control—for taking the "high" road.

Example 2:

Situation: Emily spills her milk.

Category: Someone "under my control" makes a
mistake.

New Beliefs: My children are not extensions of
my own ego self; their mistakes are not my mistakes. My children are not perfect, I am not
perfect, and none of us needs to be perfect in
order to be loved and accepted.

Mistakes are normal. Every mistake is an opportunity to learn and to grow. Every mistake is an
opportunity to laugh at ourselves.

New Script: I will not jump up out of my chair
or yell as if I have just been attacked or intentionally challenged. I will consciously remind
myself of just how unimportant this particular
incident is in the overall scheme of things. I
will say something like, "OOPS, cow kicked the
pail again!" in order to "decriminalize" the situation for everybody, especially for Emily. I
will ask Emily to take responsibility for her
accident by cleaning up her spill (and if she
doesn't clean it up perfectly, I will allow her
her imperfection by ignoring it).

Example 3:

Situation: A telemarketer solicits a donation
(during the dinner hour).

Category: Someone makes a request of me.

New Beliefs: I am not responsible for everyone else's happiness and well-being. I have boundaries; I have needs of my own and these needs may sometimes be in conflict with those of others. I cannot allow somebody else's needs to become my own simply by their expressing them to me; I cannot always subordinate my own needs to those of others. I do not need everybody to like me.

New Script: Once I have determined the nature of the call, I will immediately interrupt by saying, "I'm sorry, but we do not take solicitations of any kind over the telephone...thank you very much." Then I will hang up—and enjoy my dinner while it is still warm.

Christmas:

Situation: I feel responsible for making everybody else's Christmas the ideal it's supposed to be.

Category: I feel obligated to make everybody else happy, to take away their pain.

New Beliefs: I am not God. I am not Santa Claus. I am not responsible for answering the prayers of everybody's lingering "inner child," or for taking away the pain of all their past disillusionments, whether these be real, imagined, or projected. I am not responsible for making perfect that which no mortal can make, or attempt to make, perfect. I am only responsible for making Christmas what I need to make of it, for myself—a special occasion for honoring and renewing my relationships. Everyone else will take care of themselves, in their own way, according to their own needs, in their own time. At most, I will be a model of what Christmas can be, realistically, as a deliberate choice.

New Script: I will shop not out of guilt but out of pleasure and anticipation, and with per-

spective; I will allow myself to enjoy the
process of matching the person I care about with
a modest gift that truly reflects the sentiment
behind it; I will make notes as ideas occur to
me throughout the year in order to prevent myself
from losing those serendipitous opportunities
(which are themselves gifts) to make a truly special match. I will bake, decorate, wrap, write
cards, cook, and sing to the extent these activities bring me pleasure, not to the extent they
fulfill "duties" or allay guilt. I will ask for
help when I need it. I will let go of any piece
of the former whole that threatens to detract
from my enjoying the new whole.

Activating the New Scripts

As with making New Year's resolutions, the easy part of replacing old counterproductive scripts with productive new ones is writing them down. The real work comes when we attempt to activate these new scripts. The key word here is "work," which, the laws of physics remind us, requires energy, especially when we must deal with the force of an old momentum. Work also requires commitment, resolve, and the ability to start over—up to an infinite number of times!

However, Rome was not built in a day, Everest was not scaled in a single bound, and Hamlet was not written in a first draft. As with all other human endeavors well worth the effort, the secret to rescripting one's self lays in taking the overall task one step at a time. Here are a few suggestions you may find useful.

- **Avoid an "all or nothing" approach.**

  Avoid trying to rescript yourself in one heroic, all-inclusive effort. (In fact, if you haven't already, you may wish to add "all or nothing" problem-solving approaches to your list of old, coun-terproductive scripts.) Instead, examine the library of your old counterproductive scripts, and pull one off the shelf as a starting point. Which script you choose is not as important as the act of making the choice. Now you have a focus—a single point on which you can concentrate your considerable but limited energy and resolve.

The idea here is to work toward a success that will itself become a momentum, a source of energy, for further successes. As you build this momentum, you may find that you are able to concentrate on implementing more than one script at a time.

• Start out by consciously following the new script.

Old scripts, like old habits, tend to have a life of their own—a momentum that can only be overcome with a conscious, willful countervailing effort. For this reason, we cannot simply intend to use a new script in place of an old one in a particular triggering situation; we must instead anticipate the triggering situation and then consciously, deliberately follow the letter and spirit of the new script instead of the grooved habit of the old one. If we do this and are patient with ourselves—allowing ourselves the backslides and inconsistencies that are a condition of our humanness—the new script will gradually but inevitably become internalized and thereby automated.

Even if we are able to successfully change the beliefs underlying an old script, we will still find it necessary to consciously follow the letter of the new script. Changing the beliefs may make the overall task easier, but it will not eliminate the need for us to take conscious, willful control—and thereby allow the beleaguered child we once were to rest in peace.

• Fine-tune the new script as necessary.

Sometimes the new scripts we write and implement are not quite what they need to be. They might not be properly targeted, or they might not go far enough, or they might even go too far. In such cases, we need to make an assessment: Why is this new script not working? What do we need to do to this script in order to "fix" it?

For example, we may have recently discovered that the fundamental belief underlying one of our automated avoidance scripts is that absolutely no one in this world is to be trusted. Everyone, no matter who they are, sooner or later will betray us. The old counterproductive script we constructed on the basis of this generalized belief directed us to avoid—at least be *severely* wary of—

all intimacy, all reliance. It also placed us in an infinite loop of confirming our beliefs about the universal untrustworthiness of others. It did this by compelling us to be constantly testing all those who might try to get close to us and then measuring their inevitable shortcomings against impossible standards.

Our new script, on the other hand, takes us to the opposite extreme, in both belief and behavior. Under this script, *everyone* is deserving of our trust; hence, everyone is to be trusted—openly and completely, no matter who he or she is, or what the particular circumstances might be.

Obviously, this new script, implemented unavoidably in an imperfect world, cannot work for us either, and is, in fact, another example of the folly of "all or nothing" thinking. Indeed, how long would we suffer the inevitable consequences of this new script before we would take blessed refuge in the old one?

What we clearly need to do in this and every similar case is simply to step back, make an assessment (just as we have done in the previous paragraph), and then fine-tune our script as our best judgment directs us. For example, instead of holding the belief that everyone is deserving of our trust, and then proceeding to invest our trust indiscriminately, we can fine-tune our script to some comfortable point short of the "all of nothing" extreme.

For example, most people in this world not only are deserving of our trust but will actually tell us, in myriad ways, without any need for us to "test" them, to what degree they would like us to trust them. We will attune ourselves to their cues—we will pay attention to what they say, and how they say it; to what they do, and how they do it—and we will invest our trust accordingly. We will allow trust to grow of its own accord; we will not attempt either to make it happen or to foil it from happening.

Note: Finding the right balance between pollyanna optimism and paralyzing cynicism is not an easy task. An increasingly dangerous world compels us to be "street smart" in an ever-increasing number of "streets." Be this as it may, it remains in our best interest to avoid favoring a cynical stance over a more optimistic one. When it comes to investing trust and allowing intimacy, better that we be burned a few times than we play it too safe. We can recover from our burns; we can never recover from opportunities lost, or relationships missed—the ones we were too afraid to embrace.

In sum, rewriting the old, counterproductive scripts is potentially one of the most liberating, most empowering exercises we victims of personal or childhood trauma can undertake. It puts our adult self firmly and fully in charge of our behavior; it makes our adult self fully responsible for how we treat others, how we invite others to treat us. Perhaps most importantly, it frees the child we once were from carrying a load she was never intended to carry.

She thanks you.

The Magic Butterfly

You are sitting on the windswept knoll of your daydreams, the one you have for so long intended to visit, once you had finally sewn all the missing buttons on the tattered garments of your life. The sun is warm and healing on your face and body, freed of the pinch and nag of clothes that do not quite fit. Your damp skin is scented of the humus of your soul.

Closing your eyes, lifting your face into the full stream of the healing rays, you listen as the soft breeze whispers a timeless lullaby in your ears, the same one you longed for when you were a child, trembling beneath thin bedcovers in the slithering darkness of your terror. You feel your body growing lighter, as if invisible hands were at work behind you, lifting away the weight of too many burdens carried for far too long. A carefree thought flutters into your mind, perches on an unencumbered bough for a moment: Perhaps there are such hands, visible only to the soul, ready to reach out to all who will but allow them the possibility.

You sense something alight on your hand, a presence of little more substance than an eddy of listless air, the ticklish gossamer of a dandelion seed. "Mosquito!" you hear a voice within exclaim. "Parasite! Victimizer! Slap it! Get it before it gets you!"

But you do not slap it. Lifting your hand, intending to redirect this creature just being itself with a puff of air, you open your eyes to the full bloom of the most beautiful butterfly you have ever seen, a feast of all the colors that are, patterned in swirls and pearls of perfect symmetry.

Remaining fearlessly on your hand, the butterfly gently exercises its magnificently embroidered wings . . . down and up . . . down and up. Two jet-black filaments, standing atop its diminutive head, flex back and forth, as if in a gesture of greeting. Wiggling your nose, you return the favor.

Suddenly fluttering into flight, the butterfly circles your head, flutters away; returns and circles, flutters away; returns and circles. You rise and follow. Hard pressed to keep up with your winged guide, you pass through an unattended orchard, a field gone fallow, and enter a forest filled with deepening shadows and unsettling sounds. The chill makes you aware of your nakedness. Just when you are beginning to doubt the wisdom of your trust, you emerge from the shadows to find yourself standing at the foot of a knoll crowned with a magnificent crystal palace, glittering like an ice castle under a late-February sun. Taking a deep breath, you climb the one hundred fifty-three steps to the open portal, both sides of which, strangely, are embossed with your letter.

You follow the butterfly inside, where the uniform whiteness of the interior seems almost to transform your colorful guide into a dance of laser lights. Passing through the vaulting snow-white foyer, the butterfly leads you up a winding staircase, and into the cathedral chamber of a snow-white bedroom. You notice your letter embossed on both bedposts, and you follow the flight of the butterfly, to the door of a closet, in front of which your guide now begins to dance fitfully.

Dare you open this closet? Dare you look inside and behold what is there?

Realizing you are exactly where you are supposed to be, you grasp the porcelain knob and pull. The door sticks for a moment, from lack of previous use, then yields to your resolve. Inside, hanging in company only with itself, is the most beautiful, the most dazzling, full-length gown you have ever seen. Obviously it is tailored by an artist of incomparable skill, capable of expressing on the outside the inexpressible beauty that lies within. The gown is embroidered like the butterfly, with the very same perfectly balanced pearls and swirls of every color imaginable.

Slipping the gown effortlessly over your body, you can tell immediately that this gown was tailored for only one person in all the universe. There is not a nagging pinch, not a pinching nag. You and the gown are one.

You start to glance around the room for the butterfly, needing to express your gratitude, but it is not there. No matter. You will meet it again . . . the next time you smile into a mirror.

Being Who We
Really Are

*The pursuit of the Inner Child has taken over at
precisely the moment when most Americans ought to
be figuring out where their Inner Adult is.*
—Robert Hughes
Culture of Complaint: The Fraying of America

*This above all else: to thine own self be true,
And it must follow, as the night the day,
Thou canst not then be false to any man.*
—*Hamlet*
Act I
Scene 3, Line 75

*Writers are taught to "write what you know about."
The same advice applies to the quest for the power of
soul: Be good at what you're good at.*
—Thomas Moore,
Care of the Soul

Many of us are underdeveloped selves. Most of us are uncomfortable, anxious selves. All of us are fragmented, alienated selves. None of
us, likely—if we have gotten this far in this book—is our *true self*. None
of us is that wholly integrated, uniquely gifted, harmoniously authentic person we were intended to be.

Instead, we are an archipelago of those disconnected selves we
believe others want or expect us to be. We are a "white elephant" col-

lection of those selves we believe we simply *must* be in order to be acceptable—worthy. We are a collage of those selves we invented or fabricated when we were very young in order to secure physical and emotional safety for ourselves. We are—to be ruthlessly blunt—*fakes*.

We are to our own selves false, and the cost has been—and continues to be—enormous. Let us count just a few of the ways.

- **Some of us yearn to be engaged in "'careers'" that resonate with deep cords within us: to be potters or shopkeepers, woodworkers or homemakers, teachers or poets, veterinarians or fishing guides. However . . . .**

  We continue to pursue careers that bring us security and/or acceptability but leave us feeling increasingly empty and inauthentic. Many of us live in constant fear of being "found out" for the fakes we indeed are, while others of us cannot bring ourselves to give up the "devil we know for the devil we don't."

  We feel trapped. We feel angry and resentful. We feel dispirited and despairing. We feel we are where we cannot otherwise be; that our bed has been made for us, and now we have no choice but to lie in it.

  When people we newly meet ask us what we do, we feel a stab of shame. When they tell us what they do, we feel a stab of envy.

- **Some of us feel a vague urge to be playful and fun loving, to be spontaneous and carefree—childlike. However . . . .**

  We are not about to make damn fools out of ourselves by engaging in any unplanned activities we will end up regretting; after all, we are "the responsible ones," the ones for whom life is—always and foremost—serious business. And we are not about to earn our own wrath and condemnation by shirking duties and goals not yet accomplished; after all, the Eighth Deadly Sin is having fun before one has sufficiently earned the right to it. And we are not about to make ourselves uncomfortable by stepping onto a limb of the unknown (any place in which we are not in control).

- **Some of us feel at least the hint of a tug to connect with nature, to commune with kindred creatures, to immerse ourselves in the miracle of being. However . . . .**

For the moment at least, we are just too busy trying to cope with all the clutter and clamor in our lives—not to mention the considerable angst—to be able to yield to small gravitations tugging us in a perhaps entirely different direction. Maybe tomorrow.

- **Some of us hunger for real simplicity in our lives. However . . . .**
We are so used to—addicted to?—being overwrought, hassled, stressed out, embroiled in the crisis of the moment that, when it comes right down to it, we cannot truly imagine ourselves living any way other than the way we are currently living. Hey, this is the way it's always been, we tell ourselves; it's just the way it is. Besides, the "quiet desperation" we endure today is the price we must all pay in order to earn our way to a little contentment tomorrow; after all, "heaven" must be earned. No pain, no gain.

And, too, the more time and energy we spend just getting through the day, the less we have available for thinking about all those things we don't really want to think about; we can just continue to allow ourselves to be swept along by the currents and tides of "fate."

- **Some of us are naturally "shy" and contemplative. We prefer the quiet company of our own thoughts and introspections, we prefer the camaraderie of a few close friends, to the chatter and clamor of the throng. However . . . .**
We fear that if we allow ourselves to be true to our natural gravitation toward our interior world, people will think us unfriendly toward them, or worse, rejecting of them. Therefore, we force ourselves to be what we are not: gregarious, chatty, outgoing, initiating, action-oriented, other-seeking. We force ourselves into clothes that do not quite fit.

In other words, instead of being the perhaps materially poor but spiritually rich woodworker, shopkeeper, homemaker, or quilter we were meant to be, we may have forced ourselves into a mold that constrains our potential in those areas we have the most clay to work with, that pulls and extrudes our potential where we have the least. Ticketed passengers, we have boarded the wrong plane; invited guests, we have delivered ourselves to the wrong party; rounded pegs, we have driven ourselves into squared holes.

The cost has been, and continues to be, the simmering angst of someone caught in the eternal limbo of her own nightmare. Standing alone on stage, she must witness herself play a musical instrument she has not learned; she must deliver a speech she has not prepared; she must act a part she has not rehearsed. In front of her, in the audience, are all those people in her life on whose admiration and esteem she feels wholly dependent.

If we are truly to break free of the tethers binding us to our victimhood, we must let go of the false self we created in order to survive our troubled childhood; we must discover and embrace the unique self we were intended to be; and we must strive to use our gifts to make a contribution only we can make—to an always-welcoming creation, always in the state of becoming.

Letting Go of Our False Self

Our false self is the suit of armor we fashioned for ourselves in order to survive a childhood that, instead of being validating and nurturing, was the very opposite. It is the set of behaviors and skills we adopted in order to make ourselves pleasing to others, acceptable to others, lovable to others; and it is the set of beliefs and values we had to internalize in order to pursue and gain whatever level of physical or emotional security we needed in order to feel safe. And though this false self once worked well for us—protecting us when we were most in need of protecting—it does not work for us now. Once our suit of armor, it is now our prison, an inflexible shield of psychic iron holding us in place, weighing us deeper into the swamp of our inauthenticity.

Our false self is actually two selves mingled inseparably into one: a *love-me* self, and a *protect-me* self. Our love-me self is motivated (driven) to do or pursue whatever is required to bring us the acceptance and love we need in order to feel validated as worthy human beings and to feel integrated into the larger group or community. Our protect-me self is motivated to do or pursue whatever is required to make us feel safe from physical or emotional harm.

We see the dynamic of the false self in the addict who can never quite attain the ultimate "high" that will forever free her from her pain. She must constantly up the dosage of her particular opiate just to stay even. Similarly, the false self (entirely made up of aspects of the ego self) can never quite attain the ultimate level of acceptance or love that will forever free it from the relentless pangs of anxiety and despair tormenting it. It must constantly redouble its pursuit of emotional and physical reassurance, constantly up the ante.

Being pleasing or acceptable to Mom or Dad becomes being pleasing or acceptable to our friends and intimates, becomes being pleasing or acceptable to everybody with whom we come in more than fleeting contact; being an Eagle Scout or Blanche in the school play becomes being a lawyer or "the life of the party," becomes being a senator or a professional entertainer (ever wonder how many politicians and movie stars come from dysfunctional homes?). Not trusting anything Mom or Dad promises us becomes not trusting anything our friends or intimates promise us, becomes not trusting anything anybody promises us; getting our fair share at the table becomes hoarding our "fair share" against all hands real or imagined, becomes stuffing ourselves with our "fair share" even when we are completely and utterly alone.

Instead of recognizing the rainbow on the inside, we chase the rainbow on the outside, the pot of gold at the end, the one that will solve all our problems. And even though we pursue this pot of magic with heroic determination, running after it ever harder and harder, somehow it continues to elude us. So we run even harder! We run so hard, in fact, with such consummate focus of mind and will, we fail to see that we are a mirror image of the addict who can only free herself from her pain by turning within and facing the truth that lays there, at the end of the rainbow that arches there.

As victims of personal and childhood trauma, we can free ourselves from the distorting, tormenting constraints being imposed on us by the very armor we fashioned to protect ourselves only when we acknowledge and fully embrace who we really are. To do this, however, we must first acknowledge and let go of who we are *not*. In other words, we must acknowledge and let go of both our love-me self and our protect-me self.

For many of us, this may seem tantamount to asking us to leap from the top of a tall building into a tiny speck of a canvas held by unseen hands far below. The self we are now—the one we have been for all of memory—is the only self we know. It is the entirety of *who we are*. To ask us to give this up may feel like asking us to give up life itself.

There is, however, no "high" stakes, "all or nothing" gambit here.

There is no call for us to leap from the top of the World Trade Center into a tiny net being held by persons we have absolutely no reason to trust. There is only a call for us to take one small step at a time, at ground level.

Letting Go of Our Love-Me Self

Early in our conscious history, many of us sensed that our parents loved us at best only conditionally; at worst, not at all. In some cases, we sensed they wished we had never been born. Whatever our experience, in our child's mind there could be only one reason why our parents—those all-knowing, all-powerful god-like beings who created us in their own image—would withhold their love from us: We didn't deserve it; we weren't worthy. We were in "sin" and there could be only one way of redeeming ourselves. We had to make ourselves into the person our parents wanted us to be. In other words, we had to fabricate a love-me self.

Picking up clues from what our parents said or did not say, what they praised or did not praise, what they punished or did not punish, we gradually gained a vision (not always a clear or static one) of the mold into which we had to fit. We discovered that if we kept our room neat, for instance, and did all our own laundry, then they would praise us. If we became an Eagle Scout, or sold the most Girl Scout cookies, then they would brag about us to others. If we got all A's on our report card or made the varsity volleyball team, then they would give us a pat on the back. If we were absolutely "loyal" (kept all the family secrets safely buried in the backyard of conscious awareness), then they would withhold their withering silence from us. If we appeased dad, did whatever he asked, then he would shower us with special treats. If we aligned ourselves with mom, became her confidant and protector, then she would secretly wink at us across the room. If we became a doctor or a lawyer, then they would look at us with pride.

Our Goal. Many of us have spent the entire span of conscious memory attempting to squeeze ourselves into just such a mold, trying ever so desperately to "get it right." The more we have tried, however, the more elusive our quest—that tantalizing rainbow on the horizon—seems to have become. In the end, we have all but wholly and utterly exhausted ourselves. The time has now come for us to let go of the love-me self driving us to such exhaustion, making us chronically susceptible to the despair that inevitably fills the vacuum of such exhaustion, in order to make way for our true self to emerge from within. If we think of our true self as a coiled spring, being suppressed and diminished in proportion to the two overwhelming weights of our false self—our love-me self and our protect-me self—we can visualize our goal as doing the work necessary to remove these weights, such that our true self can then naturally stretch to its full, intended height.

The Process. The desperate child we once were is the author of our love-me self; and our love-me self is the owner, player, and perpetuator of many of those old, counterproductive scripts we discussed in the previous chapter ("Rewriting the Old Scripts"). Specifically, it owns and controls those scripts that direct our behavior toward attaining the approval or affections of people we perceive as being vital to validating our worth as a human being, or whose rejection we would find much too devastating to bear.

Part of the process of letting go of our love-me self requires that we replace the scripts owned and controlled by our love-me self with consciously crafted and directed others. More than this, however, we must also ask our adult self to take full responsibility for assessing and gaining whatever measure of validation and acceptance we truly need. In doing this, we will lift the distorted weight of this responsibility from the desperate child we once were.

The following steps are designed to help you let go of your love-me self:

- **Begin a process of coming to believe in the fundamental, inviolable, immeasurable, unstratifiable worth of all human beings.**

   Just as in the case of contract law, where it is recognized that we cannot agree to agree, we cannot simply command ourselves to supplant an old belief with a new one: "Today I believe this, but tomorrow I will believe that." All we can do is engage in some kind of process that places continuous pressure on an old belief in order to test its validity, while at the same time holding up a new belief as a possible alternative. We then simply let this process run its course.

   However, no process we set into motion is likely to lead to a real change in our most fundamental beliefs if we continue to submit to what, for us, may have evolved into a natural tendency to look almost exclusively on the mere surface of things, including ourselves, and to draw inferences largely on the basis of what we see, or do not see, there.

One way to begin a process toward believing in the fundamental, inviolable, immeasurable, unstratifiable worth of all human beings is to direct ourselves to seeing ourselves and others with our spirit mind—our "spirit eyes"—instead of predominantly or exclusively with our body mind. Our body mind sees pieces of self and makes judgments about these pieces. It decides whether each piece is a threat, whether it is useful, whether it is "one of us," whether it is "worthy." This is what it is supposed to do. Our spirit mind, on the other hand, sees the fundamental essence of something in the largest possible context and revels in the miracle of its intrinsic beauty. While the body mind frowns at warts and blemishes, the spirit mind weeps in awe of the encompassing smile.

Great, but how do we direct ourselves to see with our spirit eyes? It's not easy, especially for those of us who have been taught how to see by the great shamans of Madison Avenue. But here is one example: The next time you encounter someone you find physically repulsive, perhaps someone who is morbidly obese, let your body mind run rampant with judgment. After it has had its fill, consciously ask your spirit mind to take over. Focus on this "ugly" person's eyes. Look at nothing else.

What do you see? What do you feel?

• **Tune in to the love-me self in others.**

There are at least two good reasons for us to make the attempt to tune in to the love-me self in others. First, it is difficult for us to see ourselves as we actually are—the stark reality of our love-me selves—without looking into some kind of mirror. Observing the love-me self in others can be just such a mirror. This technique, in fact, is essentially what the anthropologist uses when he observes the behavior of other cultures, and what the zoologist uses when she observes the behavior of other social animals. Both are using the behavior of other groups as a mirror in which to see our own behavior. (Back in the early 1960s, this technique was used, often squirmingly so, in the movie Mondo Cane to mirror the behavior of "civilized" man in the behavior of both other social animals and more "primitive" human societies.)

Second, widening the scope of our observation beyond our own behavior allows us to assure ourselves that we aren't "the only ones." We are not alone in being influenced by, if not largely controlled by, the lingering needs of our desperate former child self.

You may wish, therefore, to stand back and take notice when, for example, someone tends to perform, achieve, or exaggerate in order to be the center of attention; when someone tends to be chronically ill, incessantly woebegotten, or forever beleaguered with "problems'; when someone tends to compromise their sanctity, their sovereignty, or their authenticity in some way in order to win the approval of others. You may wish to speculate on what is really motivating the person at the next table who is talking loud enough for everyone in the room to hear; on what is really motivating the person who seeks adulation through election, elevation, or applause; on what is really motivating the person who allows herself to be exploited or mistreated by "intimate" others.

As you are observing and making your speculations, ask yourself: Is this me I am watching? Is this who I want to be?

Note: In observing others, there is always a danger of falling into the old traps of making judgments about those we are observing and inventing a hierarchy of relative worth that allows us to perceive ourselves as standing on a higher plane or of being self-servingly selective in who we choose to observe. Falling into these traps is a natural tendency not just for those who may feel especially vulnerable, but for all humans, whatever their individual makeup or history. We are all predisposed, in other words, to being lured and seduced by the age-old, time-proven siren songs of the secular self, who is always looking for a way to justify elevating itself to a position of preeminent worth and therefore survivability. Forewarned is forearmed.

• **Draw a portrait of your love-me self.**
Another way we can capture our love-me self, such that we can then stand back and acknowledge its full reality, is to draw a portrait of this very distinct aspect of ourselves. We can accomplish this by asking ourselves certain key questions. For example, we might ask ourselves: Do I have a tendency to try to get everyone to like me? Do I shy away from or avoid situations in which I am afraid I will fail to meet others' expectations of me? Do I tend to

withhold, hide, or misrepresent aspects of myself that I am afraid people will use to judge me unworthy or unacceptable? Do I have a tendency to be overly generous—to give too much, to say "yes" too often, to volunteer to do too much? Do I have a tendency to adjust my likability, how I am presenting myself in the moment, on the basis of what I sense in people's moods and body language? Do I have a tendency to hide feelings that I am afraid might be unacceptable to others? Do I have a tendency to make choices on the basis of what other people are likely to think about them, and therefore about me? Do I have a tendency to dress not so much "for success" as for acceptability? Do I have a tendency to be fiercely loyal, even to persons or institutions that mistreat me? Do I seek to be the center of attention in some way (by over- or under-achieving; by talking too much or too loudly; by having one "illness" or "problem" or crisis after another)?

Asking yourself these and similar inquiries, write down an intimate portrait of your love-me self, one that transforms one-word "yes" or "no" answers into simple, but direct declarations. For example:

—I tend to withhold, hide, or misrepresent aspects and information about myself. that I am afraid people will use to judge me unworthy or unacceptable.

—I have a tendency to be fiercely loyal, even to persons who mistreat me.

—I seek to be the center of attention by having one crisis after another.

• **Symbolically dissociate your mature adult self from your child-created love-me self.**
   For human beings, symbols and symbolic gestures or rituals can be very strong medicine, giving not only concrete meaning to abstract ideas and notions, but form to the spirit of possibilities and potentials (flesh to the word). What's more, the power of the symbolic is equally accessible to all, limited only by our own individual imagination (or willingness to use it).

Here is one way you may wish to enlist the power of the symbolic: Using a current photograph of yourself, draw a mask over your face, using a red marker or crayon, such that this mask consists of two large hearts, one heart drawn over each eye (making yourself into a sort of "Love Ranger"). Keep in mind that your eyes are the windows of your soul, to your true self. Now, on the back of your photograph, write down all the aspects of your love-me self that you acknowledged in the previous step (save some room—just in case!) You now have a symbolic representation of your love-me self.

In dissociating our love-me self from our adult self, we want to avoid any approach that appears to hold the promise of instant gratification; human beings simply do not effect change on the fundamental level by snapping their fingers. Therefore, instead of tearing up your symbolic love-me self and casting all the pieces to the wind (a favorite "workshop" activity), gradually move your symbolic love-me self away from your "center," represented by a central room in your home (bedroom, kitchen, living room), until it is physically too far away from you to be or feel like it is a part of you. For example, you might move your symbolic love-me self from your living room to your doorway; then, after perhaps a few days, from your doorway to your yard (any location immediately outside where you live); then from your yard to some point about a block away; then from about block away to perhaps a half-mile away. Continue this until your love-me self attains a physical distance from you that feels like complete severance (you will know it when you feel it).

Letting Go of Our Protect-Me Self

As children, in addition to inventing a love-me self, whose job it was to make ourselves worthy of being validated and included, many of us also invented a protect-me self, whose job it was to give ourselves (at least the illusion of) the tranquillity, the predictability, and the physical safety we were not otherwise getting. Instead of focusing on discovering and developing our gifts, on taking small risks into the unknown of our potential (and having fun doing it), on learning how to invest trust and nurture intimacy, we focused on developing control and manipulation skills, on building "walls" around us, on making ourselves invisible, on devising stratagems, on learning how to function as an adult (how to be "street-wise" in our own homes), on ensuring that we get "our share," on making ourselves feel powerful, on avoiding even the smallest risks.

We came to believe we needed safety, security, comfort, and predictability above all else, and so we came to internalize these goals as our preeminent, driving values. And what we came preeminently to value, we have preeminently sought to attain. We have sought to make ourselves invisible enough, removed enough, peripheral enough, so finally we would feel safe. We have sought to acquire enough, to accumulate enough, to horde enough, so finally we would feel secure. We have sought to eat enough, to pleasure ourselves enough, to numb ourselves enough, so finally we would feel comfortable. We have sought to control enough, to direct enough, to manipulate enough, so finally we would feel our world to be predictable.

So it has been, so it remains.

Our Goal. Many of us have squandered enormous amounts of our precious time and energy seeking to free ourselves from the threat—always present to the child self we continually revert to—of physical or emotional harm. However, the more time and energy we spent trying to protect ourselves from this threat—by avoiding risks, by making ourselves invisible, by acquiring possessions and/or the means to yet more possessions, by pleasuring ourselves, by controlling events and people around us—the more elusive our goal became, and the more exhausted we became. We must now let go of the protect-me self that is so utterly depleting us, in order to make way for our true self to emerge from within. Again, if we think of our true self as a coiled spring, being suppressed and diminished in proportion to the two overwhelming weights of our false self, we can visualize our goal as doing the work necessary to remove these weights, such that our true self can then naturally stretch to its full, intended height.

The Process. As in our love-me self, our protect-me self is the owner and operator of many old, counterproductive scripts we discussed in the previous chapter ("Rewriting the Old Scripts"). Specifically, it owns and operates those scripts that direct our behavior toward avoiding risks and making ourselves invisible, acquiring and accumulating material forms of security, pleasuring or numbing ourselves, and controlling and manipulating the people and events around us.

In other words, our protect-me self manipulates the scripts that attempt to bring us the freedom from harm that we so desperately needed to attain—to *feel*—when we were children.

Letting go of our protect-me self, then, requires that we replace the scripts created by our protect-me self with new scripts created by our adult self. This means we must pass to our adult self the full responsibility for assessing and gaining whatever measure of freedom from harm we truly need. We must, in other words, finally lift the weight of this adult responsibility from the desperate child we once were.

The following steps are designed to help you let go of your protect-me self:

- **Begin a process toward letting go of fear as a controlling force in your life.**
  Franklin Delano Roosevelt (in truth, his speech writer) once reminded us that "We have nothing to fear but fear itself." Roosevelt invoked this ancient truth in the face of demons emerging from the despair and desperation of a rapidly deepening economic crisis of the 1930's. Other icons of authority have since invoked this old truth, most recently in the face of fear demons unleashed by ever-increasing, ever more-indiscriminant acts of terror and mayhem.

  Roosevelt's injunction is well worth repeating here, too, especially for those of us who were "terrorized" at a time in our lives when we were most vulnerable and dependent. For us, fear became not just a distraction or complication but the central organizing principle in our lives, leading us not to life, liberty, and happiness, in the form of personal authenticity and fulfillment, but to safety, security, and comfort, in the form of invisibility, materialism, risk aversion, pleasure-seeking, and numbness.

  Our problem now is that, although we are no longer the wounded, helpless child we once were, continually terrorized by wolves dressed in sheeps' clothing, we still behave as if we were. We still seek that last, ultimate layer of safety that will bring our Great Wall to a thickness that will protect us from all those threats lurking in the shadows of both our reality and our imagination. We are still so utterly preoccupied with this futile quest that many of us have yet to even begin to discover who we really are and what this miraculous experience we call "life" is really all about. Clearly, it is time to get past the roadblock of our fear, so we can get on with our journey "home."

For many of us, however, our journey home is complicated by the special nature of our fear. We see this same complication in hostages rendered into a childlike dependence by their terrorist captors. Over time, these hostages tend to identify with their captors—to become sort of "terrorist codependents." Those of us who have been "terrorized" by childhood neglect or abuse—and then by our own imaginations—similarly tend to become sort of "fear codependents." In effect, our fear becomes an angry god on whom we tend to focus our entire lives. In order to sway it from casting us into an ever deeper rings in the Dante Inferno of our imagination, we must constantly appease and accommodate it—never challenge or defy it. For us, then, fear is more than just a roadblock we must either climb over or detour around; it is the entire expanse of our universe.

On some level—the level of our spirit mind—we know that this angry god (this terrorist captor) we have allowed to become our lord and master is really no god at all. It is as mortal as we are—created to exactly the height and stature required to keep it in charge. It is a man standing behind a curtain, frantically pushing levers and pulling strings to keep a certain facade or false reality fully intact. To be free of its hold, its spell, we need only pull the curtain back to reveal the very same truth Dorothy discovered in the Land of Oz and that Pogo discovered in the pages of another universe paralleling our own: "We have met the enemy and he is us."

Think about this the next time someone invites you to do something you've never done before. Instead of giving in to the usual impulse to keep yourself safely invisible, out of harm's (humiliation's) way, you can reach out and pull the curtain back from the little man pulling the levers. Instead of coming up with a lame excuse, you can accept the invitation without a moment's hesitation—and show up for the event five minutes early.

• **Tune in to the protect-me self in others.**
As in the case of our love-me self, observing the protect-me self in others can help us see the protect-me self in ourselves.

Widening the scope of our observation allows us to assure our-selves that we aren't "the only ones." Many adults in our culture are controlled in the present by the lingering needs of the desperate child they once were.

You may wish to stand back and take notice when someone places himself in a position either of absolute control (as in teaching) or of complete invisibility (as in sitting at the very back of the classroom); when someone would rather walk five miles out of her way than risk a confrontation; when someone saves everything because "you never know when you might need it"; when someone indulges himself with food, drink, or sex during periods of stress or disappointment; when someone is more interested in the longevity of a job than in the nature of the job itself. You may wish to speculate on what is really motivating the person who becomes a physician even though he doesn't particularly like people; on what is really motivating the person who must eat when she cannot possibly be "hungry"; on what is really motivating the person who seeks positions of power and authority; on what is really motivating the person who always "plays it safe." (Note that the love-me self and the protect-me self can express their "needs" by leading us in a common direction. For example, we may run for political office to win the attention of others [including Mom and Dad] and to gain power [security].)

As you observe and speculate, ask yourself: Is this me I am watching? Is this who I want to be?

A word of caution worth repeating: In observing others, there is always a real danger of falling into the old traps of making judgments about people we are observing, of inventing a hierarchy of relative worth that allows us to perceive ourselves as standing on a higher plane, or of being self-servingly selective in who we choose to observe. Falling into these traps is a natural tendency not just for those of us who may feel especially vulnerable, but for all Homo sapiens, whatever their individual makeup or history. We are all predisposed, in other words, to being lured and seduced by the age-old and time-proven siren songs of the secular self, who is always looking for a way to justify elevating itself to a position of preeminent worth and survivability.

• **Draw a portrait of your protect-me self.**

As in the case of our love-me self, we can also capture our pro-tect-me self, such that we can then stand back and acknowledge its full reality, by drawing a portrait of this very distinct aspect of ourselves. One way we can accomplish this is by asking our-selves certain key questions.

— In situations in which there is a choice, do I tend to choose more on the basis of safety than on the basis of opportunity?

— Do I tend to feel anxious whenever I am in a situation in which I am not in control (for example, when stuck in traffic, or when someone else is driving)?

— Do I tend to feel stress or anxiety as hunger, or as "horniness"?

— Do I tend to be motivated by (perhaps even obsessed by) money. Do I view it—what it can do or get for me—as securi-ty?

— Do I tend to view formal education almost exclusively as a means to a living, rather than as a means to enlightenment and discovery?

— Do I tend to come up with lame excuses to avoid placing myself in anxiety-producing situations?

— Do I tend to gravitate toward groups within which I know I can be in some comfortable measure of control?

— Do I gravitate toward professions that place me in a position in which I am not likely to be challenged?

— Do I tend to make myself invisible in any situation in which I might be singled out and exposed?

Asking yourself these and similar inquiries, write an intimate portrait of your protect-me self, one that transforms one-word "yes" or "no" answers into simple but direct declarations.

—In any situation in which there is a choice, I almost always choose the safer route over the one that best matches my interests and my personality.

—In any classroom situation, I tend to sit in the back of the room, and to avoid making eye contact with the teacher, whose presence I feel as a constant threat.

—I cannot bear for more than a few increasingly painful moments any situation in which I am not in control; I become more and more anxious, claustrophobic.

—I would not walk five but twenty-five miles out of my way to avoid confrontation.

—Money not only attracts me like a bear to a pot of honey, it turns me on!

• **Symbolically dissociate your adult (true) self from your protect-me self.**
   As in the case of our love-me self, symbols and symbolic gestures or rituals can be very strong "medicine." You may wish to use this medicine as follows to help dissociate your adult self from your protect-me self.
   Using a current photograph (portrait) of yourself—not the same one you used for symbolically dissociating your adult self from your love-me self—draw a mask over your face, using a black marker or crayon: two large shields, one shield over each eye. On the back of your photograph, write down all the aspects of your protect-me self that you acknowledged in the previous step. You now have a symbolic representation of your protect-me self.
   Just as you did to your love-me self, gradually move your symbolic protect-me self physically away from your "center," represented, again, by a central room in your home, until it is too far away to any longer be—to feel—a part of you.

Discovering Who We Really Are

Nature's primary strategy for ensuring the survival and progression of life is *diversity*. From this basic stratagem flows the myriad instances of shape and form that grace the earth in any particular milieu (swamp, rain forest, desert, back yard), in any particular epoch (Precambrian, Jurassic, modern, today). In every time and venue there are all manner of flora and fauna, genus and specie, group and individual. In our time and venue, there are also all manner of races and instances of Homo sapiens: black and white, tall and short, quick and slow, artist and artisan, you and me.

From our point of view, some species and instances may be more important than others. Cats may be more "important" than dogs, for example; or my cat might be more "worthy" than your cat. From Nature's point of view, however, none of these myriad groups and instances of shape and form is any more valuable or worthy than any other. Each variety and each instance contributes equally toward the perpetuation and progression of life as a whole, just as every cell and every organ in the human body is of equal value relative to the overall perpetuation and progression of the larger organism—and of the species as a whole.

In other words, from Nature's point of view, no individual or category of living thing is inherently of negative worth. No individual creature or species is intrinsically pathological, evil, second-rate, or "more" or "less." Seen through Nature's "eyes," the community of life is simply a "level" community of difference.

From this difference—this rich diversity of difference—comes all change; from this change, all true "progress."

Complementing this diversity strategy, inseparably interwoven with it, is the strategy of *survival of the fittest*. Under this strategem, Nature bestows individuals and categories with different "gifts" (characteristics and abilities), then casts them into the local "pond" to sink or swim. Those individuals who survive get to make others in their own image; those who don't get, at best, to perpetuate their image as a fossil on a nondescript layer of limestone. In other words, Nature puts a variety of actors on stage, in a variety of roles. Those who "work out" get to perform night after night; those who don't get "the hook." There is no compassion here; only expediency.

Which brings us to Us.

In addition to being given a diverse array of gifts of individual function, including unprecedented intellectual abilities, we humans have
been given the additional gifts of self-awareness and free choice. We
were given these powerful gifts, especially the latter two, to use to
adapt ourselves in diverse (virtually limitless) ways to ever-changing
conditions. In other words, more than any species before us, or con-
current with us, we have been given the ability (and the responsibility)
to willfully determine and to diversify our interactions with our environment, with other creatures, with each other—and with ourselves.

What this means on the level of everyday life is that we humans have
been granted the power to choose to be authentic (true to our individual and special uniqueness) and therefore to know the harmony, the
joy, the fulfillment that flows from "being to thine own self true." The
flip side of this power is, of course, the ability to be inauthentic—to fulfill not the purpose for which we were uniquely designed but a purpose
that can only lead to dissonance.

On the individual level, the dissonance that flows from inauthenticity translates into anxiety, emptiness, and, ultimately, into despair. On
the broader level, that is, on the species level, it translates into social
upheaval, environmental degradation, and, eventually, into planetary
catastrophe. On this level, the jury is still out on us. We're still swim-
ming, but one can sense an ever-increasing level of flailing and
foundering. We're still on stage, but one can sense the presence of the
hook.

However, you and I are not responsible for, and certainly not in control of, the overall fate of our species. We are in charge of only our own.
Our concern, therefore, is at the individual level. Our focus is diversity
and difference at this level; responsibility and choice at this level.

As victims of personal or childhood trauma, you and I have experienced perhaps more than most the terrible consequences of pursuing
an inauthentic life, a false self. Our lives have virtually been defined by
the dissonance of inauthenticity—relentless anxiety, gnawing emptiness, crushing despair, debilitating exhaustion. It is time now for us to
move past all this dissonance by discovering and becoming our true
self—that one-of-a-kind constellation of true needs, true gifts, and true
personal characteristics that, as a whole much larger than the sum of
its parts, makes us who we are and defines what we have to contribute.

Just as each crystalline snowflake is unique in all the universe, and is
of equal worth in gracing the world into which it falls, so too is each

one of us human beings—when, that is, we give ourselves the opportunity to actually *be* this unique person.

At this point, there is danger that our demon fear will rear its ugly head and remind us who's in charge. It may do this by telling us that becoming our true selves ("whatever the hell that is") would be tantamount to pushing the reset button and wiping out the only persona we've ever known. We'd essentially be self-inflicting ourselves with a lobotomy. The truth is, of course, that our demon fear is not in charge, *we* are. And becoming our true selves is not a matter of flipping an "all of nothing" switch and suddenly replacing one reality with an entirely different one—abruptly changing night into day. It's simply a process.

This process requires no more of us than that we discover what our true needs are, what our true gifts are, and what our true personality characteristics are. If we're standing on the shore of our possibilities, we can then push our canoe out into the stream and go with the flow. If we're already paddling, but against the current, we can simply stop paddling and allow ourselves to backslide to where we need to go. If we're in the wrong stream altogether, we can paddle ashore and portage (hard work, but manageable) to the stream of our true self.

Discovering Our True Needs

As human beings, we are largely motivated by tensions, like those of stretched rubber bands, between what we need (or think we need) and what we have (or think we have). We feel such tensions as a sort of hunger that develops when the cavity in which we store our reserve of a needed "substance" becomes depleted. By causing us discomfort, sometimes even pain, this feeling of hunger serves to capture our attention, such that we then direct ourselves, consciously or otherwise, to engage in whatever activity or activities might be necessary to replenish the substance that has become depleted. The greater the depletion, the greater our hunger, the greater our discomfort, the more robust will be our efforts to obtain the needed substance.

The most obvious example of a need that alerts and motivates us through a feeling of hunger is our need for food, which manifests itself each time our stomach grows empty and begins to feel uncomfortably hollow, sometimes even painfully so. However, we can apply this same hunger-as-motivator model to the entire host of our other needs as well, including our need for love, our need for security, and our need for joy. Indeed, when we are depleted of external love, do we not feel lonely; do we not crave attention and reassurance from others? When we are depleted of safety and security, do we not become anxious; do we not crave islands and self-sufficiency? When we are depleted of joy, do we not feel angst; do we not crave pleasure or numbness?

If we examine the entire spectrum of our needs, we see that each of the three major facets of the self has an identifiable set of vital needs: Our physical self has a certain set of vital needs, our emotional self has a certain set of vital needs, and our spiritual self has a certain set of vital needs. Some people tend to draw "hard" boundaries around these needs so they can place them in the proper category ("a place for everything; everything in its place"): physical, emotional, or spiritual. They also tend to assign relative values to individual needs as well as to the categories. The truth is, of course, that none of these needs has a hard boundary that exclusively separates it from all others, that is, that places it in only one category. And no need, or category of need, is more important than any other.

Consider, for example, our need for food. This very basic need seems to be exclusively physical in nature and also to be pre-eminently important. We eat food (substance) to maintain our body (substance). If we don't eat, we die; if we die, none of our other needs matters. If we will look a little deeper, however, we will see that our need for food also has both an emotional and a spiritual dimension. We will also see that this need, however basic and vital, is no more important, within the context of the whole self, than are our seemingly subordinate needs for humor and for "connection."

For example, picture yourself slurping a spoonful of steaming-hot soup on a cold winter's day, after spending an hour or two shoveling out the driveway. Or place yourself in a hot shower after returning to civilization from a three-day camping trip in the woods. Are you experiencing anything besides the physical warmth and flavor of the soup. Are you feeling anything deeper than the steady stream of hot water on your skin, and the tingle of shampoo in your hair? Is what you are feeling *exclusively* physical in nature?

Consider, too, the celibate monk, self-exiled in a walled retreat from all the material and sensual "temptations" of life, attempting to meditate, pray, deny, and self-flagellate his way to a state of perfect spiritual bliss. What assumption is he operating under? Can fulfillment or happiness be achieved exclusively within the spiritual realm of human experience?

Consider, too, the investment banker, self-exiled in his penthouse office from everything that might remind him of his mortality and his humility, working 16-hour days to achieve the deal that will make him richer and more renown than any other wheeler-dealer on earth. Under what assumption is he operating? Can human happiness be achieved exclusively within the material realm of human experience?

In summary: To be authentically our true selves—to achieve the inner harmony that is the source of all lasting joy—we must recognize and address the needs that flow from *all* the dimensions of the self. And we must address these needs concurrently, holistically, and equally rather than separately, linearly, or hierarchically.

Under "normal" circumstances, most of us would go about meeting our needs without having to give much conscious thought to what we were attempting to accomplish, just as a mother, under "normal" circumstances, goes about meeting the needs her infant makes unambiguously known to her. In other words, but for certain intervening forces, we would naturally be inclined to simply paddle downstream in the natural flow of our authentic selves, undistracted by any "need" to do otherwise.

However, those of us who experienced personal or childhood trauma, and whose needs were distorted by an upside-down reality, do not now function within "normal circumstances." Instead, we function within a context that feels as if we were the only wet nurse in a whole nursery filled with screaming, wailing infants, each demanding our full attention to meet its separate need.

Nothing we do is ever quite enough to satisfy the myriad hungers we feel within us—to quiet all those screaming infants. No matter how much achievement, fame, praise, applause, adulation, or fierce membership we suckle them with, it is never enough. No matter how much money, job security, material accumulation, emotional distancing, self-reliance, physical strength, or practical knowledge we spoon down their throats, it is never enough. No matter how much work, food, drink, sex, exercise, entertainment, drugs, or travel we fill their silver cups with, it is never enough. The distracting hunger remains, often painfully so; the wailing continues, often maddeningly so.

The underlying problem is not, of course, that our inner self has in fact dissociated into a legion of wailing infants in a state of arrested development. Our needs have simply been tilted out of balance, thereby tilting us out of balance—just as a disproportion of wet and soggy towels in the spinning tub of the washing machine render the whole machine out of balance. We are in dissonance because we have been favoring some of our needs to the neglect of others—in some cases, to the complete and utter neglect of others. Our immediate goal, then, is to remind ourselves of the full range of our needs, including any of which we may have lost sight. We can then attend to all of them in proper balance.

The following exercises are designed to help you discover the full range of your needs:

- **Draw a behavior profile that typifies the activities you tend to engage in and the choices you tend to make.**

  Valleys exist because mountains do; the higher the mountain, the deeper the valley. The same is true of our needs. When certain of our needs mount into a lofty peak, certain others sink into a shadowed valley. If we will look to our mountains, therefore, we will discover our valleys. For example, if we look to the mountain that is our need for "entertainment," we might discover the valley of our need for connection.

  Some of us, however, may not be ready to confront all the Himalayas in our lives in so direct a manner, not to mention all the Death Valleys. We may wish to use a more indirect approach:

  Activities. Sit down in a comfortable chair and simply describe, on paper, an average day, week, or month in your life.

  — How do you spend your time? What activities (mental as well as physical) do you engage in? What activities do you avoid?

  — Do you spend time "grooming" for the day? Do you fuss over what you are going to wear?

  — Do you spend any time meditating or examining your life?

  — Do you look forward to your job(s)? What specific activities do you perform at your job? Do you commute to this job? If so, how far and with whom?

— Do you read the newspaper? If so, which section do you read first? Second?

— What do you do with your "free" time?

— Do you watch television? If so, which programs do you watch?

— Do you read books or magazines? If so, which ones?

— Do you correspond with anyone? If so, with whom and what is the nature of your correspondence?

— Do you exercise or work out?

— Do you plan trips?

— Do you daydream? If so, what about? Romance? Escape? Revenge?

Interactions. Describe your interactions in relating with other people.

—Who are these people?

— What is the nature of the communications between you and them (frequency, length, content, tone)?

— What is the nature of your relationship with your boss? With other "authority figures" in your life? (Be sure to include your interactions with your family.)

Purchases. Finally, describe your purchases and how you spend money.

— What kinds of things do you buy? What kinds of things do you aspire to buy?

— Do you pay cash, or do you charge?

— Who pays the bills?

— Do you run up the balance on any of your credit cards?

Your goal is create as complete a description of how you normally spend your time and energy as you can—what you do, the choices you make. Of course, what you are actually doing here is writing down your needs "signature," a profile of "hidden" information that reveals the particular configuration of needs that underlie and motivate your behavior. Have you ever watched a movie in which the Private Investigator goes through the trash of an unsuspecting subject in order to get a "profile" on this person? Indeed, the trash we leave behind is simply another way we all unsuspectingly divulge who we are. (For the fun of it, go through your own trash and make a list of everything you find there.)

• **Identify the "payoff" for each activity or choice you identified in the previous step.**
We've identified what we do, what we choose; now let's identify the quid for each quo. Go back through the list of typical activities and choices you recorded in the previous step and ask yourself what the primary gain or benefit is (or appears to be) for each one. In other words, identify the "payoff." For example: Is the primary reason you hold your current job that it allows you to be who you really are, to do what you really like to do? Or that it pays the bills and provides health insurance? Or that it brings you respect and prestige? Is the primary reason you write letters simply that you enjoy this ancient art? Or that you like to get letters in return? Or that you don't like to talk face to face or on the telephone? Is the reason you own a forty-two inch, high-resolution stereo TV that you simply could not live without it? Or did you want to get a better look at all those creatures great and small on PBS's *Nature*. Or did you want to be the first among your peers to have one? Or did you want not to be the *last* one of your peers to have one?
Let go. Avoid letting your ego self attempt to soften, deny away, diffuse, filter, rationalize, or otherwise edit the payoff that seems most strongly to claim dominion over a particular activity or choice. If ever there was a time for complete honesty, this is it.

- **Identify the dominant need behind each activity or choice you identified in the previous step.**

We know what we do, what we choose; we know what payoff we get; now let's identify what need we are feeding with each payoff. Looking a little deeper into the quid-pro-quo's you developed in the previous step, identify the need that appears to be the prime cause (motivator) behind each payoff you have identified. You are not required to get this exactly right; simply speculate as best you can on the basis of the information you have supplied to yourself. Use the following examples:

Primary Payoff
Current job pays the bills (with enough left over to finance an annual two-week escape to McBrigadoon).
Primary Need
Security (Instead, find security in who you really are.)

Primary Payoff
Spending considerable time grooming every morning and fussing about what you are going to wear gives you confidence about your appearance.
Primary Need
Acceptance (Instead, focus on the beauty of your interior appearance, which will be reflected in your exterior appearance.)

Primary Payoff
Spending a considerable amount of your time and money on various forms of entertainment is a distraction from all those things you do not wish to think about, much less deal with.
Primary Need
Pain "medication" (Instead, renew and energize yourself to face up to whatever pain is present.)

Again, let go. In each case, put down what most strongly feels to be the primary need being fed by the payoff each activity or choice is rendering for you.

Once you have finished your list, study it closely to see if any particular needs seem to stand out or dominate your behavior and/or choices. If they do, make note of these, for these are the wailing infants in your nursery, the domineering Himalayas in the landscape of your needs.

• **Identify any other needs you may have.**

In the previous steps, we have gently guided ourselves toward identifying the peaks that dominate the landscape of our needs. In doing this, however, we have also revealed the valleys—those needs we have been overlooking. For example, in asking ourselves why we hold the job we have, did we not reveal a need to derive satisfaction from our work moment-to-moment, rather than, at most, once in a blue moon (do these even exist!)? In asking ourselves why we avoid new experiences or unfamiliar situations, did we not reveal a need to be free of the fear that is fencing us in our own back yards? In asking ourselves why we buy certain things, did we not reveal a need to fulfill ourselves in a deeper, more lasting way? In asking why we pursue the particular relationships we have, did we not reveal a need for risking intimacy over safe superficiality?

Did we not also reveal a need to be an integral, essential part of something larger than ourselves? Did we not also reveal a need to feel authentically able and powerful, self-assured in the efficacy of our own gifts? Did we not also reveal a need to make sacrifices and contributions that are their own reward? Did we not also reveal a need to feel comfortably attired in the wardrobe of our own person, instead of always chaffing in someone else's hand-me-downs? Did we not also reveal a need to look toward the moment of our death without dread or fear—to know in the present that when this moment arrives for us we will be able to greet it with a smile?

Make a list of every valley (neglected need) you can see. Standing atop the peaks, you should not find this all that difficult. Don't be alarmed, however, if a tear or two drops to the page to punctuate your truth.

Either we are addressing the entire range of our needs or we are not. Either we are addressing our needs in proper proportion (balance) or we are not. If we are not, then we are stuck, and there we shall remain until such time as we set about unsticking ourselves.

TOM FITZGERALD

If we must to-our-own-selves-be-untrue in order to get what we think we need, if we must kill off our spirit (a piece at a time) in order to get what we think we need, if we must obsess in order to get what we think we need, then we don't really need it. If various pied pipers spend millions of precious dollars trying to reinforce our notions about what we think we need, luring us into their air-conditioned lairs with barrages of sly advertisements, disingenuous testimonials, and subliminal seductions, we still don't need it. We need only what we know we need, and we all know.

Discovering Our True Gifts

Nature diversifies all of life—the various faculties and characteristics of all living things—across bell-shaped curves. Consider height, for example. Only a few of us are very short; just as few are very tall. The great majority of us are lumped into an average or near-average height. Overall, the distribution of human height neatly takes the form of a bell-shaped curve. The same is true of all other innate human characteristics and faculties: body type, aggressiveness, shyness, native intelligence, artistic ability, etc. The median is the most; the extremes are the least.

This strategy satisfies two crucial survival goals. These goals seem to be in conflict but actually are not: *continuity* (preservation) and *experimentation* (change). Continuity is needed to preserve what works; experimentation is needed to provide what might work if environmental conditions should change.

It is at the extremes of the bell-shaped curve that Nature experiments, and in the middle that she preserves. In other words, she experiments only with great caution, making, for example, very few of us extremely short or extremely tall (or extremely aggressive or extremely meek, and so forth). By lumping the vast majority in the middle of the curve relative to any particular characteristic (height, aggressiveness, bone-size, agility, wit, whatever), she ensures that the greatest number will survive under current (and anticipated) conditions.

If conditions should change for some reason (sustained droughts, for example), the species is prepared, because at least a few of its members are "experiments" whose particular configuration of characteristics and faculties may allow them to survive under the new conditions. Under sustained drought conditions, for example, species members who are

158

significantly smaller and therefore in need of less food and less water may survive while larger kindreds die off. If the droughts become permanent, so likely will be the change in the species.

You and I have different places on a whole host of bell curves. I may have a big-boned, 6'2" stature, may have wavy blond hair and green eyes, may have a natural inclination toward shyness and introspection, may have a natural ability to see the forest through the trees, may have a natural ability to translate abstract notions into tangible pictures. In contrast, you may have a medium-boned, 5'7" stature, may have straight rust-red hair and blue eyes, may have a natural inclination toward gregariousness and communion, may have a natural ability to engage with others and win their trust, may have a natural ability to translate your inner beauty into external color and form. If we connect all the points of our position on all these bell curves, we each become a snowflake—a unique crystal of human characteristics and faculties.

Nature shuffles the gene deck and we all come out a different hand—each a unique "true self."

In this regard, some of the characteristics and abilities making up a particular true self may be more visible than others, just as some of the component stars in the Big Dipper or in Orion may be a little brighter than others. However, no one "gift" is any more important than any other, because, from Nature's point of view, it is the constellation as a whole that defines the unique purpose of each individual and gives each constellation its "identity."

There was a time (at least an intention) when the core purpose of the liberal education was to create a context in which each individual could discover her unique "identity"—her particular gifts—and come to understand the purpose that these gifts collectively defined. In this nurturing environment, each individual would be urged and encouraged to develop her gifts as she came to recognize and accept them, and to follow whatever path they collectively gravitated her toward.

In today's secularized world, we do not have benefit of this kind of examining, validating, mentoring education. In fact, we have quite the opposite. We have choruses of voices urging us to travel in every direction except the one for which we are uniquely suited. We have internalized voices (especially from our dysfunctional past) constantly telling us the "truth" about ourselves, and we have a multitude of external sirens whispering "sweet nothings" in our ear, urging us away from being who we really are, toward being the doctor, the accountant, the

MBA, the lawyer, the engineer, the politician, the corporate executive, the entrepreneur, the "10," the acceptable "somebody" we simply must be in order to "make it" (to make ourselves acceptable to others, to fit ourselves into a popular mold).

The only voice telling us the truth about ourselves is the only one that can—the one that speaks from the oracle within. This lone voice, however, is very likely being drowned out, even as we read these words, by the shrieks and shouts of a thousand other, competing voices, internal and external. These are the familiar, authoritative voices to which, unfortunately, many of us have become all too prone to heed.

For many of us, then, discovering our true gifts is likely to be no easy matter. But it is a task we simply must undertake. If we do not, we essentially condemn ourselves to remain forever stuck in the swamp of our victimhood, to suffering perhaps the greatest of all horrors—realizing at the moment of death who we really were, what our gifts truly were.

The following exercises are designed to help you discover your true gifts:

- **Tune in to the voice within.**

  Unfortunately, many of us associate pleas or urgings to "tune in to our voice within" with such New Agey refrains as "be in the moment" and "all is one," or with such other seemingly nonsensical or empty refrains as "the media is the message" and "a rose is a rose is a rose." Say what? If we take a fresh look, however, we will see that our voice within is not the kind we can hear with our "body ears," not the kind who speaks to us from the throne room of our reason or from the library of our memory.

  Our inner voice does not speak to us in words, in discrete units of sound and meaning that we can put down on paper. Rather, it speaks in waves or surges of feeling, in currents of resonance and harmony. It is the only medium of meaning to which we humans have access that can carry the massless weight of pure truth. Words—particulate, bounded, inexact—simply cannot do this.

  Our inner voice is more music to fall into resonance with than it is imperatives to fall into lockstep with.

  In tuning into the voice within, therefore, we must make a leap—from the world of the reducible, the concrete, the static, the cognitive—to the world of the whole, the fleeting, the dynamic, the intuitive. However, we must also do something that for many of us may represent an ever larger, wider, chasm to cross. We must accept that we, and only we, hold the truth of ourselves. Only we can hear and feel the silent voice of this truth. Others may be able to surmise bits and pieces of our truth, from catching glimpses of it here and there, as one surmises the presence of diamonds, rubies and sapphires by the color of their glitter; but they can never grasp the whole of it. Nor should they try. This is not their responsibility; it is ours alone. What others (parents, teachers, mentors) can do for us is encourage and empower us to turn inward and feel the flow of our truth. They can give us permission to give ourselves over to this truth. They can assure us they will accept us no matter where they truth might lead us.

Suggestion: To begin a process of tuning into your voice within, immerse yourself in a few moments of deep tranquillity each day. You might sit in a room by yourself with your cat on your lap; you might go for long walks where there are no automobiles and few people; you might jog along a shaded path. The idea is to place yourself in an environment that allows the natural rhythms of your physical self to harmonize and become one with the deep chords of your spiritual self.

Allow your conscious thoughts ('roof chatter') to take you to wherever they seem to need to go in the moment; do not fight them, do not try to control them. Let them play themselves out. When your inner landscape finally quiets to the liquid stillness of an autumn dusk, take a deep breath—hold it—let it out of its own weight. Silently ask your oracle within: Who am I? What are my gifts? What are the stars in my constellation? To what would I naturally gravitate—flow—if I were to let go of the push and pull of all the shoulds and oughts (the "false gods') in my life?

If I were to *really* let go?

Closing your eyes, listen to the music that is the answer.

• **Take an inventory of your natural talents and abilities.**

Keep an erasable list of all the talents and abilities you discover in yourself. Use a pencil to record the individual entries, so you can readily make changes and prevent yourself from inadvertently locking yourself into a profile that is not entirely the product of your inner voice. In fact, the voices you listen to in the early stages of capturing your profile are more likely to be the old, familiar ones—the ones that have been telling you who you are from as far back as you can consciously remember—than they are your true inner voice. Give yourself time to get past all the dogs barking in the night. Sooner or late you will hear a purring emanating from deep within your soul.

If you have been instilled with a strong sense of "false modesty" (an aversion to being the center of attention) that does not allow you to acknowledge your gifts directly—that is, you can't make statements such as, "I am a natural artist" or "I have a natural ability to create harmony with color and texture"—then rewrite the old, counterproductive script that is blocking you from acknowledging your true self, or make an end run around this block by acknowledging your gifts indirectly. For example, you could capture the same meaning contained in the two statements above by phasing them in more indirect terms, such as: "I like to play with colors and textures, arranging and rearranging them until I feel the combination is just right."

In fact, you may wish to approach this entire exercise by beginning each item in your list with the words "I like to" instead of the words "I am" or "I have."

I like to put puzzles together.
I like to work with young children.
I like to make pictures with words.
I like to grow things.
I like to sew my own clothes.
I like to help people avoid making mistakes I have made.
I like to discuss ideas with kindred spirits.
I like to be with animals.
I like to build things with my hands.
I like to talk to people.

Note, however, that after you have made your list, you can (if your dare) take each one of the activities you have identified as something you like to do and translate it directly into a "gift."

I have a natural ability to solve problems.
I have a natural ability to work with (nurture) young children.

I have a natural ability to create pictures with words.
I have a natural ability to grow things. (I have a "green thumb.")

Sometimes translating what we like to do into who we really are simply does not work. Sometimes we like to do things for which we do not necessarily have a natural aptitude or gift. For example, we may like to play the guitar but at the same time be nearly tone deaf (as in the case of Jack Benny and his violin, though spuriously so), to the chagrin of all who may have little choice but to listen to our "music." However, this seeming paradox is relatively rare, for the simple reason that we humans naturally enjoy doing what we are naturally adept at doing, just as the otter naturally enjoys sliding down slippery slopes on its naturally accommodating belly, and the red-tail hawk naturally enjoys riding afternoon thermals on its naturally buoyant wings. Indeed, because this seeming paradox is relatively rare, when it does happen, you may wish to step back and ask yourself if the particular activity in question is something you really like to do, or is, in fact, just another lingering facade of your false self, bent on distracting you until the very last.

To help you authenticate a natural attraction to each activity in your list of things you like to do, close your eyes and picture yourself actively engaged in each activity. In each instance, ask yourself: What am I feeling? Who am I doing this for? What am I getting out of this? You may discover, for example, that, instead of feeling transcendent and spiritually attuned when playing the piano, you actually feel uptight and anxious. You may discover that you took up the piano when you were nine not to please—to *be*—yourself, but in order to please parents who openly revered the people who played the piano at the Saturday night bashes they hosted.

If we dare to know and to acknowledge the truth about ourselves, it cannot other than set us free.

Discovering Our True Personality

Some of us tend to bristle whenever we hear someone declare anew (sometimes seemingly "in our face') that "biology is destiny." However, there is a tough truth riding the back of this slogan that will not be bucked off and that we must all recognize and come to terms with if we are truly to allow ourselves to know the truth about who we really are. To wit, we are all dealt a unique "hand" of physical and personal traits from the set of all possible combinations. This unique hand constitutes no less a determining factor in our eventual fate than the innate characteristics of redness and singleness create for a red, single-petaled tulip. Indeed, no matter how much the red tulip might try, it can never actually become a white double-petaled tulip.

Likewise, if we are 5' 2", we can never make ourselves 5' 7", or 6'2", or 7'4". If we are innately tone deaf and/or digitally clumsy, no matter how many hours we dutifully pound out notes at the keyboard, earnestly striving to be a virtuoso, we will never be a virtuoso. If we are chronically shy and introverted, no matter how much we might force ourselves to be gregarious and outgoing, we can never actually be gregarious and outgoing. If we are prone to gather information experientially rather than cognitively, no matter how much we may try to force ourselves to be "voracious readers," we are never going to be voracious readers. (We may buy a lot of books, out of guilt, but we will never read them all.) We are each biologically (and uniquely) bounded.

Our biological boundary is not, however, our prison. It is instead the fullness of a unique opportunity, a plot of ground sufficient for us to sink our roots deeply into and grow into the fullness of the one-of-a-kind bloom we were meant to be.

The key here is, of course, "choice." Opportunity is simply another word for choice. Because we humans possess the unique gift of what we call "free will" (the power to paddle upstream as well as down), being who we were meant to be is always a choice. If it were otherwise, there would be no need for this guide book and no need for either of us to be having this discussion; we would be as the tulips that grace our April gardens, each wholly and beautifully its own self without the intervention of free will. This would be no opportunity—only destiny. To make this choice, however, we must be fully aware of all the natural aspects of our true personality—all the individual cards that have been dealt to our unique hand. We must know our unique traits, inclinations, and dispositions. In other words, we each must know the fullness of our true personality, which the following suggestions are intended to help you discover.

- **Play Word Association using the physical and personal aspects of yourself as the subjects.**

The Word Association Game, as a form of brainstorming, can be an effective means of deactivating the various valves and filters our ego self uses to deny us access to the full truth about ourselves.

As a "warm up," start out by listing on paper the physical aspects of yourself that define who you are as a corporal presence and thereby differentiate you from others; for example: height, body type, complexion, hair, eyes, nose, feet, hands, wrinkles, fingernails, stretch marks, and the like. Use "What do I look like?" as the primer that allows you to draw the full truth to the surface. If necessary, study yourself in a mirror, both up close and from a distance, in order to keep the flow going.

Strive to compile as complete a profile of your physical self as would be necessary to differentiate you from any and all other members of the race on the planet, to, say, a visitor from Mars. Your physical self is not exactly an aspect of your personality, but going through this exercise in regard to the "harder" aspects of yourself can be useful in helping you become a more objective observer in regard to the "softer" aspects.

Once you have completely (and objectively) profiled the physical aspect of yourself, move on to your personality. Write down all the words and phrases that come to mind when you ask yourself: What kind of person is <u><your-name></u>? How do other people see this person? How would they describe her?

For example:

She tends to wait for other person to make the first move in any situation in which she feels like a stranger or an outsider.

She tends to be even tempered rather than prone to yo-yoing between mood extremes.

She tends to procrastinate until a deadline is breathing fire on the back of her neck.

She tends to be private about her feelings and personal life.

She tends to gather as much information as possible before she makes a decision or takes a stand on an issue.

She tends to solve problems by talking about them rather than by going off by herself to ruminate about them.

She tends to visit every store, to investigate every possible selection, before she makes a decision on a purchase.
She tends to be able to adapt gracefully to new situations, to make easy transitions.
She tends to be easily distracted by, sometimes even paralyzed by, all the possibilities.
She tends to need a great deal of "quiet time."
She tends to prefer bright colors over either earth tones or pastels.
She tends to be able to deal with only one task at a time. ("Don't talk to the cook!")

Brainstorming is an especially useful technique here because it allows us the measure of objectivity we need to make our profile as complete and honest as possible. The effect is to separate ourselves into an "object self" and an "observer self" and to put as much distance between these two selves as possible. The greater we can manage to make this distance between object self and observer self, the more successful we are likely to be in perceiving and describing the salient personality traits of our true self.

If we allow ego self to make judgments at any point, to reactivate those valves and filters that deny us full access to the truth about ourselves (in other words, to invoke the harsh scolds and shamings of our false vanity), all will be for naught. We will simply end up profiling the false self we are attempting to let go of.

This is no time for false vanity. Write it down as it is.

• **Profile yourself by means of a formal personality indicator.**

One of the most liberating aspects of discovering who we really are—especially if we perceive ourselves as being "different" in a "less than" sort of way—is discovering just how many of our personality traits are *innate*, and how *unalone* we are in sharing these traits with others. A tool that is especially effective in bringing us this kind of discovery is the formal personality indicator.

Personality indictors are used by professional vocational counselors to help them assess an individual's likelihood of being able to function comfortably within a given environment. However, they can also be used to bring to the foreground in a single, inclusive frame the full constellation of our personal self. What's more, by normalizing characteristics about ourselves that we may currently be reluctant to accept, much less embrace, they serve to detoxify or deshame these characteristics.

One of the most widely known and readily available of these indicators is the Myers-Briggs Type Indicator, originally developed by an astute (and compatible) mother-daughter team back in the 1950s. (Another popular indicator is the Enneagram, pronounced "any-a-gram.")

By asking us a series of key questions, the Myers-Briggs Indicator measures our preferred way of functioning or being in each of four major areas, where each area consists of a continuum between two extremes: Introverted-Extroverted; Intuitive-Sensing; Thinking-Feeling; Perceiving-Judging. Based on our apparent preference in each of these four areas, the Indicator then places us into one of sixteen possible personality types, where each type has a distinctive profile of personality traits or tendencies. (The Enneagram uses nine personality types.)

For example, if our preferences indicate that we tend to operate more by introversion (internal stimulation) than by extroversion (external stimulation), more by intuition than by sensing, more by feeling than by thinking, more by perceiving than by judging, the Indicator would place us under the INFP personality type. Personality traits and tendencies consistently characteristic of this particular personality type include the following:

We are warm and enthusiastic, but only toward those we know well.
We tend to be idealistic, with passionate conviction.
We are tolerant and flexible, but never to the point of compromising a loyalty or an ideal.
We have little need to impress or to dominate others.
We find it difficult to express our deepest beliefs and feelings.
We are highly motivated by tasks that involve making a contribution to human understanding, happiness, or health—often to the point of perfectionism.
We are insightful and visionary.
We need to see all the possibilities beyond what is present and known.

We tend to be facile with language, to be persuasive and creative.
We tend to be attracted to careers in counseling, teaching, litera-
ture, art, science, and psychology.
We tend to suffer a sense of inadequacy from "failing" to suffi-
ciently close the inevitable gaps between our lofty ideals and
our actual achievements.
We tend to become overly sensitive and vulnerable from not being
able to find an appropriate medium for expressing our ideals.

Of course, exercises of this sort—aimed toward revealing the fullness of our true personality—are not perfect, because they cannot be. They can only render us approximations, in the manner of the portrait painter. Such approximations, however, can go a long way toward helping us discover who we really are— come to terms with who we really are. Even if we are hardcore skeptics at the outset, we are likely to be gently swayed by the results in the end. Many have resisted; many have fallen.

If you are at least open to falling yourself, you can find the Myers-Briggs Type Indicator, as well as volumes of literature about it (descriptions of its personality types especially), at most bookstores and libraries. If you have trouble finding it, or a similar indicator, contact the vocational counseling (or placement) office at the nearest college or university.

Step by step, we have discovered the fullness of the unique being we were intended to be. We have discovered our true gifts, our true needs, and our true personality traits. However, discovering who we really are is not necessarily being who we really are. To be who we really are, we must set who we really are into motion. In other words, we must *do* who we really are.

Doing As We Really Are

We do as we *believe* we are, not necessarily as we *really* are. In fact, our behavior is largely our beliefs about ourselves in motion. If we believe we need to be gregarious and outgoing in order to be a "normal" (therefore an acceptable) person, even though we do not feel comfortable acting in this role, then we will focus our time and energy on forcing ourselves to be gregarious and outgoing, to the neglect of seeking the solitude that draws us like swallows to Capistrano. If we believe money and material wealth will bring us the security we were denied in our childhood, then we will focus our time and energy on enduring (getting through yet another week of) a job that kills off a little bit of our spirit each day, to the neglect of our need to make a real contribution. If we believe duty and responsibility will bring us the personal validation we never got from our parents, we will focus our time and energy on accepting and carrying out, even to the point of utter exhaustion, every request for aid or assistance made of us. In other words, if our sense of self is based on a set of false beliefs, we cannot other than behave falsely, inauthentically (unto our own selves untrue), and hence unfulfillingly.

What we know in our hearts and must now face at this critical juncture is that no amount of money or wealth, achievement or success, career or vocation—no amount of anything gained at the behest of our ego-driven false self—can ever bring us anything more meaningful or lasting than brief surges of well-beingness, followed by ever more desperate cravings for ever larger doses of the same drugs. If ever we are to achieve the kind of personal fulfillment and inner peace we seek, we must let go of all the old beliefs that compel us to devote our lives to seeking ever larger doses of the wrong "stuff." We must embrace a new set of beliefs that center around being who we really are—being unto our own selves true. We must, in other words, come to believe in the unique self we really are—the true needs of this self, the true gifts of this self, the true personality of this self—so that we can naturally, authentically, and therefore fulfillingly do as we really are.

However, as we have previously suggested, we cannot change our beliefs—supplant an old, deeply ingrained set of beliefs with an all-new, largely "untested" set of beliefs—simply by snapping our fingers or waving a magic wand. Or can we?

Does the belief always have to precede the behavior, or can the behavior precede the belief? If "believing is seeing" is as true as "seeing is believing," might "doing is believing" be as valid as "believing is doing?" Doing, in fact, may be a way of allowing ourselves the opportunity to feel the sense of authenticity and inner peace that only comes with conforming our behavior to the truth about who we really are.

In truth, we do not need to surgically remove our old beliefs about ourselves and replace them with a full set of new ones in order for us to begin to "do" as we really are. We can, in fact, place ourselves on a path suggested by what we appear to have discovered about who we really are, and then walk a few steps down this path without in any way committing (condemning!) ourselves to it. When we try on a new pair of shoes and take a few steps around the store in them, we are not committing ourselves to buying them. We are simply trying on their "truth," to make sure it won't give us blisters.

Here are a few suggestions to help you get started.

- **Think big, but start small.**

A task that can appear to be essentially reinventing ourselves can easily be perceived as too scary or too overwhelming to undertake. This is especially true, of course, for those of us who tend to see through eyes colored by fear, or who tend to think in terms of "all or nothing," or whose need to be in control renders making transitions very difficult (if not impossible).

As always, the secret to not talking ourselves out of a journey before we get started is to look no further than the next footfall or handhold. This strategy prevents us from becoming intimidated or overwhelmed. It also allows us to be surprised by just how attainable our goal really is and by how rewarding the journey is in itself. Perhaps most importantly, it allows us to make course corrections. It gives us the time and space we need to make sure the new pair of shoes we're trying on really fits.

Therefore, instead of telling yourself that in order to be your true self you must make a precipitous "leap of faith"—quit your job tomorrow, sell the house and move to northern Utah, start teaching the kids at home, start building Shaker furniture without benefit of electrified tools, start growing all your own food,read all of the canon classics by December 31, 1999, toss out all three television sets and both VCRs, give at least half your life's savings to the Salvation Army—you might simply wish to enter a process that sets you in motion down a new path one step at a time. You may, in other words, wish simply to allow yourself time and space to acclimatize yourself to what may be unfamiliar territory (rain forest, perhaps, versus treeless plain), and time and space to confirm the overall suitability of this new territory relative to who you really are. Indeed, who among us gets it right every time, never has to backtrack out of a box canyon, never has to cut her losses and try another hand?

It may turn out that we actually do quit our job and move to Utah. If we do this tomorrow, however—if we act precipitously and attempt to take full and immediate control of our ultimate destiny—we will likely defeat ourselves before we even get started (as so many of those who made such abrupt "be free—be me" transitions back in the tumultuous '60s found out). Easy does it...one step at a time—all for the right reasons. Our goal is to change our compass heading; it is to paddle in a new direction. It is not to instantaneously "beam" ourselves to a Garden of Eden awaiting us just over the horizon of our angst.

To help you keep a measured approach, then, you may wish to avoid making any rigidly defined, all-or-nothing "five-year plans" that lock you into a narrow view of where you need to go and what you need to do in order to get there. As the central planners in the former Soviet Union found out, such rigid efforts to plan several years into the future almost always fail—for the same reason all rigid bodies of dogma eventually fail: they do not allow for self-correction. They eliminate all possibility of amending, adjusting, reconsidering, of choosing other possibilities. These are possibilities that our limited vision cannot even begin to foresee in the present and that can only come our way by virtue of our opening ourselves to them. Indeed, the only real control any of us has over our destiny is not in limiting the possibilities, and thereby narrowing ourselves, but in making the best possible choice among all the possibilities that present themselves to us in the moment.

Instead, therefore, of focusing your attention on formulating a whole new reality—getting it all right all at once—you may wish to focus your attention on the one best choice you can make in the moment, this moment, that will contribute, however modestly, to bringing your overall behavior (what you tend to do, what you tend to choose) into alignment with who you really are (your real needs, your real gifts, your real personality traits).

For example, you might choose to start using your true gifts in "stolen moments," that is, outside an 8:00-to-5:00 job that allows you little opportunity to use these gifts by pursuing a hobby or a sideline business on a modest, but consistent basis. Or you might choose to give yourself permission to make a decision on the basis of your "gut feeling" instead of on the basis of "hard data" and endless iterations of cognitive analysis. Or you might choose to make contact, eye and verbal, with the (until now, invisible) janitor at work. Or you might choose to linger at the dinner table this evening to listen to what's really on your children's minds. Or you might choose to pause long enough from a frenetic schedule to revel in the restorative beauty of a regal elm tree or a unique cloud formation. Or you might choose to write a brief note to a teen-aged pen pal badly in need of someone's unconditional attention. Or you might choose to give yourself permission to make a decision slowly and methodically, even in the face of the possibility of being judged "indecisive" by certain impatient others. Or you might join up with the local Habitat for Humanity organization this weekend to help build a house for someone who, up until you and others got involved, had absolutely no hope of ever owning her own home. Or you might choose to enter marital therapy with your spouse, instead of continuing to distance yourself from yet another person you perceive as having "betrayed" you. The possibilities are, of course, as numerous and as diverse as you allow them to be.

- **If you are trapped by "financial responsibilities," start plotting (plodding!) a way out.**

Our debts, present and promised, tether us to our past, to our false self—to our old ways, our old beliefs, our old path. To the degree we are burdened with debt, and thereby bound by it, like Gulliver in Lilliput, we will find it difficult to take even small steps down a new path.

Burdening ourselves with debt can be symptomatic of a misguided effort to fill spiritual emptiness with material pleasure (to satisfy that relentlessly gnawing hunger deep within us, by "feeding" it an ever bigger house, an ever bigger car, an ever bigger stereo, an ever bigger vacation, an ever bigger wardrobe, an ever more drastic liposuction). It can also be symptomatic of an effort to purchase ourselves a palpable sense of importance and meaningfulness under the misguided belief that the more things we have, the more important and meaningful we must be—in our own eyes and in the eyes of others. Whatever the reason or reasons behind it, however, the debt we accumulate is not the by-product of the choosings and doings of our true self, since our true self has no need of anything that any amount of debt might bring us.

This, however, is no time either to lament our debt or to beat ourselves up for having accumulated it. It is simply time to get out from under it. Unfortunately, though, there is no easy way to accomplish this, especially if the needs and values that motivated us toward accumulating this debt have likewise been instilled in those who are currently financially and materially dependent on us. Indeed, in order to get truly free of our debts, not only must we face a painful withdrawal syndrome similar to the one every chain-smoker or addict cannot avoid in order to get free; we also must deal with the potentially agonizing question of whether it is fair for us to unilaterally "change the rules" for those in our lives who will inevitably be affected by any withdrawal from material dependency that we choose to make. In other words, we must deal with the complication that not only is getting out of debt unavoidably going to discomfort us; it is also unavoidably going to discomfort others, including those who may already be a source of guilt for us.

No matter what our particular complications are, though, getting out from under is indeed do-able. There is always a way—a process that will work best in any particular set of circumstances, such as how much present debt we have accumulated, how much debt we have promised (for example, in promising to send our children to the "best" colleges, to give our daughters a "big" wedding), the nature of the dependencies that our debt has fostered, and so forth. Because these circumstances can vary widely, so can the process.

There is one component that all such processes must share in order to bring about the desired results: Each must stand on a firm, unshakable commitment to simplicity—not only to the concept of simplicity, but to the reality of simplicity. In other words, each one must be focused on downsizing (to a smaller house, a smaller car, a smaller stereo, a smaller vacation, a smaller wardrobe), on sacrificing (letting the Joneses win), on paying off debt (in full), and on lowering our own and others' expectations. Without such a commitment, as in the case of going on a diet to lose weight permanently, whatever mind games we play with ourselves, they are not likely to have the desired effect.

Suggestion: You may wish to put in the form of a written commitment (contract) any intentions you choose to make in regard to extricating yourself from debt, along with the reasons you are making such a commitment. You may then wish to do two very important (strategic) things. First, you may wish to share your commitment with every person who is going to be directly affected by it. Doing this will not only make it more difficult for you to renege on your commitment (by placing your pride on the line); it will also respectfully give everybody involved an opportunity to understand the changes you are making and to support you (eventually if not immediately). In fact, in the near term do not be surprised if affected others try to punish or "guilt trip" you into breaking your new commitment, for such is the way of human nature.

For example:

I, Thomas L. Fitzgerald, do hereby commit myself to entering a process toward freeing myself from the indebtedness and material attachments that are currently distracting me from fulfilling my true purpose in this life. I am entering such a process because I have come to realize that I cannot truly be happy until and unless I address these real needs, including my need to make personal contributions and sacrifices toward others, and until and unless I let go of my "false" needs, including what has been, until now, an insatiable need to win, buy, or ingratiate the acceptance or admiration of seemingly every other soul on this planet . . . on their terms.

Second, you may wish to renegotiate any and all contracts (implied or explicit) that you currently hold with all those linked others in the web of your life who are potentially going to be affected by your commitment. If you do not do this and simply impose on these others the specific terms of the process you put into place for getting out from under, you are likely to alienate the very people you need to support, cooperate with, and grow with you. You will also deny yourself an opportunity to benefit from their ideas and suggestions on how best to achieve your (and perhaps their) overall goal.

If you are not comfortable conducting negotiations, you may wish to enlist the services of a third party, someone who is neutral, trusted by all parties, and well-versed in the art of stepping through mine fields.

Of course, bringing others into your commitment and into the process for fulfilling this commitment involves letting go of trying to control the reactions of these others and, even more, trying to control the overall outcome. Without the one, there is neither.

(Hint: If you are so deep in the abyss of debt and obligation there appears to be no way out, pick up a copy of *Your Money or Your Life: Transforming Your Relationship with Money and Achieving Financial Independence,* by Joe Dominguez and Vicki Robin.)

• Make every choice a fully conscious, wholly deliberate one.

To help us truly do as we truly are, we should strive to make every choice on a fully conscious, wholly deliberate basis. And we should do this not just in regard to the "big" choices we face, but in regard to every "little" one as well. In fact, when it comes to becoming authentic, there is no such thing as a little choice. As in being noble, compassionate, or loving, either we are or we are not; the size of the context is immaterial. We only deceive ourselves when we set up a hierarchy of authenticity, when we assign quantities of relative worth to individual acts so we might more easily rationalize a conveniently narrow focus.

To help you make every choice a fully conscious, wholly deliberate one, you may wish to ask yourself the following questions as a way of bringing to the forefront all the information your conscious mind needs in order to be truly deliberate.

• Will this choice help me meet my true needs?

To help you answer this question, you may wish to look back at both the list you made of your true needs and the list you made of your "false" needs.

• Will this choice help me use my true gifts?

To help you answer this question, you may wish to look back at the list you made of your true gifts.

• **Will this choice help me be my true person?**

To help you answer this question, you may wish to look back at your list you made of your true personality traits.

If you find yourself confused or conflicted, ask yourself one additional question: How does this choice feel? How do I feel when I project myself into the reality of this choice? Do I feel resonance; or do I feel dissonance? If you are not sure whether what you are feeling is dissonance or simply what may be a natural fear, talk to someone. Use a neutral third party as a sounding board with which to hear the deep chords in your thoughts and feelings more distinctly.

Caution: If any choice you make ends up steering you in the "wrong" direction, instead of lapsing into merciless self-flagellation, simply (reflexively) stand back and ask yourself: "What have I learned from this experience? How can I use what I have learned to get myself back on track—perhaps even ahead of where I might otherwise have been?"

Our wisdom comes from the mistakes we make, from the genius we employ to overcome them, not from the number of whip marks we inflict on ourselves. Every mistake is simply an opportunity disguised in shame's clothing.

Afterword:
Many Are Called

The mass of (wo)men lead lives quiet desperation. What is called resignation (victimhood) is confirmed desperation.
—Henry David Thoreau
Walden

Each one of us has, at this very moment, all the resources we need to get to where we need to go. Each of us has the ability, the power, the opportunity, and the time (the space we make available through value choices). Unfortunately, even though we all have all the *resources* to get to where we need to go, not all of us have the *gumption* to get there. The pluck. The stamina. The discipline. The utter indomitability. Indeed, even though we all get the same call, the same invitation, some of us simply do not have the staying power to do the *hard work* necessary to achieve perhaps the only kind of redemption we can ever know.

Hence, sooner or later, we must all ask ourselves: Which one am I?

In conjunction with this question, we might also find ourselves asking: Do I really have the power to bring about real change in my life?

If you harbor any doubts concerning this latter question, take a moment and try this: Sit down and rewrite (or tape) *one* of those old, counterproductive scripts you created many years ago in order to help you survive particular situations in your childhood. Write or tape this new script, then physically place yourself in the situation for which it is intended (walk onto a "real stage," in other words). Instead of unconsciously allowing yourself to be controlled by the old script, consciously follow the new one. As you are using this new script, take a mental step backward and ask yourself: Who's in control? Who's going to be in control—real control—from now on?

Or, sit down and visualize what childhood was probably like for someone who, as an adult in your life, has caused you great and lasting harm. Pick a particular incident, real or imagined. Ask yourself: Is this person inherently and irredeemably a monster, or "But for the grace of God goes anyone of the rest of us?"

Or, take a walk and make eye and verbal contact with everyone you meet, including any "street people" you may encounter (who, by the way, are far hungrier for your acknowledgment than they are for your loose change). Ask yourself: Is not what I am giving here exactly what I am seeking?

Or, simply go out, right now, and a get a book on personality type indicators (e.g., *Do What You Are* by the Tiegers two) from the local library or bookstore and take the "test." Ask yourself: Is the person in this mirror the same person I have for all these years been trying to mold myself to be?

In other words, pick a *single,* specific, manageable action, and do it now rather than tomorrow or when you have "more time" or when you are "in the mood." Then stand back and watch the currents and eddies of still air you set into motion grow, evolve, and transform into an earth-drenching, atmosphere-cleansing, life-renewing thunderstorm.

One final thought: Though context is everything, it is nothing without perspective. Perspective is what we derive from context when we consider the whole of something as opposed to only a (selected) piece or portion. It is the source of all real humility, all lasting hope. Perspective is the giant that dwarfs those bully moments of discouragement and despair that are inevitably a part of any effort to remake ourselves in accordance with our intended image. It is the wide-angle lens that reminds us of the full picture whenever we narrow our focus to the point we can no longer see every step backward as part of the next step forward.

Some say that timing is the key to success in the stock market. Others say that it is buying and holding. Still others say that it is buying when everybody else is selling. The truth is, of course, that they are all right, for they all share the same faith in the overall outcome, the same perspective. They all know that playing the stock market is not going to be a smooth ride, that there are going to be as many downs as ups—that some of those downs are even going to feel like a roller coaster out of control. However, they also know that the overall trend over time is inevitably going to be *up*. They know this because they all stand back to view the context in the whole, instead of allowing themselves to focus on or be captured by the eighty-four point drop of a single day. And they do not do this only once, but over and over again. They stand back to take stock (so to speak) whenever they temporarily lose the ability to see every step backward as simply part of the next step forward.

Many are called . . . .

Daily Reminders

Happiness is the quality of the moment; the quality of the moment is the quality of ourselves—the depth of our wisdom, the size of our heart, the lushness of our soul. We cannot be truly happy, unself-consciously happy, on the superficial levels of self. Not money, office, conquest, achievement, sex, fame, food, travel, revenge—even beating the system—can bring us anything more than fleeting flashes of ecstasy. These flashes are bombs bursting in air, temporarily transforming darkness into artificial day. Happiness is an ember glowing within, warming us evenly, moderately, taking no notice of itself. Happiness is the soft incandescence of a soul at peace with itself, with all else.

Happiness is not finally finding a pot of gold at the end of a rainbow; happiness is sharing a pot of hot soup with a fellow traveler.

If you would be happy, my friend . . . .

1

Strive to accept, to love, to give without condition or agenda. In committing ourselves to a life of spontaneous compassion, we assure ourselves of receiving everything we will ever really need.

2

Keep your expectations grounded in your reality. Inflate your dreams, but with your own breath, not with someone else"s helium.

3

Judge every opportunity, every possibility, every choice against whether it will add to or diminish the cordwood of your self-regard. Go with what you know will always feel warm and cozy, even on the coldest of deep-winter nights.

4

Know the difference between self-esteem and self-confidence. Self-esteem is what we give our children when we love and accept them without condition. Self-confidence is what we give our children when we allow them to make mistakes and try their wings.

5

Plan out the morning but leave the afternoon to chance. It is the berry we happen upon in the field left fallow that always tastes sweetest.

6

Strive for perspective. Step back and ask yourself: "Just how important is this anyway? Does this really matter?" Peer down on the clutter of your life from the summit of your cumulated wisdom.

7

Choose the company of upbeat friends and let the whiners and nay-sayers go their own miserable way. Play the dirge only for the dead.

8

Know the difference between religion and spirituality. Religion is a room with a door; spirituality is everything else.

9

Beware the demands of membership. To the extent we adhere to one group, we exclude ourselves from all others.

10

Beware the counsel of the credentialed. The cell is not biology; knowledge is not wisdom.

11

Beware all doctrines marketed as the last word in received truth. All truth is provisional, and no oracle among us can make it otherwise.

12

Accept your limitations and go with your strengths. Strive to be the one-of-a-kind miracle you were meant to be, not some wishful image in the mirror you think you should be.

13

Live within your means. The quality of life depends not on the quality of the things you possess, but on the quality of you.

14

Risk mistakes, the humiliation of error. Anyone who has observed a child realizes failure is the primary means by which all human beings learn and discover, whatever their native or gendered gifts. Safe is for the sorry.

15

Share your thoughts and feelings with others; listen to theirs. Allow yourself to discover how very much alike—in flaw and in fault, in heart and in soul—we all truly are.

16

Pursue at least one labor of love on a daily basis. We can make it across any desert of soul-searing emptiness as long as we have at least one oasis to drink from each day.

17

Leave perfection to those who must use its impossibility as an excuse to do nothing.

18

Keep a plant in the window, a pet by your side. Allow yourself the depth of connection known only to those who commune with life in all its kindred forms.

19

Be open to the need for change. When we allow fear to close our mind to the painful truth about ourselves, we sow the seeds of terrible regret.

20

Question even the best of good intentions. Well-meaningness is no assurance of well-beingness.

21

Set goals but look to the journey for joy. Our foot prints are the moments in which we live.

22

Base every decision on the very best information you can find. Most bad decisions are not the result of bad thinking, but of good thinking applied to bad information.

23

Say no when no is what you need.

24

Define your own likes and dislikes; apologize to no one for what makes you comfortable. Leave fashion to those who do not know who they are.

25

Attend to your health as you would your grandmother's china. Take responsibility for becoming a burden to no one, including yourself.

26

Invest your trust in others, but follow no one in blind faith. The Pied Piper takes many forms.

27

Strive to accomplish at least one success each day, however small, no matter how leaden the skies weighing on your soul. Shining your shoes for the first time in a year is not too small a success.

28

Leave the rat race to the rats. There are as many alternatives as there are dreams, as much courage as there is will.

29

Worry if you must, but only about those matters over which you are the goddess of the moment. Fret does not get.

30

Ask for help when you need it, offer it when others do. We are interdependent creatures all; we cannot make it alone.

31

Be swift to voice complaints, as swift to apologize for errors. Leave nothing unsaid that requires no more of you than the courage to say it.

32

Strive to become aware of why you do what you do, why you need what you need. Strive for self-control. Self-control is all we have to determine our own fate, but we cannot control what we do not understand.

33

Accept defeat with grace. What defeat gracefully acknowledged is not the greater victory?

34

Allow yourself a few moments alone each day, without exception—out of dwelling, out of work place. Take a walk; ponder the miracle of being able to place one foot in front of the other.

35

Leave fame and fortune to those who must believe happiness lies with the envy and adulation of others. Why reach for the pot of gold when it is the rainbow we are after?

36

Allow anger its due. Unresolved rage is a darkened mind, a poisoned heart, a shriveled soul.

37

Be aware of the prisms through which your mind's eye peers. Too often we see but a distortion of what truly stands before us.

38

Learn to laugh at the clown stumbling around in the center ring of your serious self. In our constant bumblings, we are delightfully comical creatures all.

39

Own the consequences of each transgression, each mistake. Discover the magical healing powers of an apology freely given, genuinely felt.

40

Know the difference between pleasure and happiness. Pleasure is a flashy car, a fat wallet, a full stomach; happiness is an act of sacrifice, an act of courage, an act of kindness.

41

Beware of all philosophies that promise deliverance from anything other than ignorance.

42

Remind yourself during those inescapable moments of hopelessness and despair that you possess, always and undiminished, the greatest power any mortal can ever possess: the power to choose, the power to strive, the power to overcome.

43
Visit the house of fear, but do not dwell there. Remain only long enough to be reminded of just how strong you truly are.

44
Forgive even the unforgivable. Revenge is allowing ourselves to be injured by the injury, the dog to bite its own tail.

45
Remind yourself during those inescapable moments of worthlessness and insignificance that the odds against your coming into being were so astronomically enormous as to make you a virtual impossibility. Yet here you are, in all your glory.

46
Allow yourself second chances; as many as it takes. Who among us learned how to walk on our very first try?

47
Listen to the teachings of others, but heed only those that resonate with deep cords within. Accept nothing on blind faith alone.

48
Strive to discover in the dawn of your uncertain tenure on this earth the unique purpose for which you were uniquely gifted. Tarry not until the hour of your final thought.

49
Wait not for happiness to be delivered to you. Not parent, not spouse, not state, not god owes us the gift of happiness (or anything else); if we are to receive happiness in this world, we must deliver it to ourselves.

50

Avoid trying to plan and control all the events and outcomes of your life. It is not manipulation that gets us to where we need to go; it is the particular horse we choose to harness to our carriage.

51

All said and done, only one simple truth truly matters: One's life can only be as bright as the enlightenment of one's mind, as full as the expansiveness of one's heart, as lush as the fruitedness of one's soul.

52

Play not to win, but for the struggle. The sweat is the victory.

Appendix A.
Suggested Readings

Though fundamental to our well-being and fulfillment as sentient, willful creatures, this mysterious essence we call "spirituality" tends to be elusive and therefore much misunderstood and sometimes even abused. One effective, readily accessible way we can all enrich our notions about it (what it is; what role it plays in the human experience) is to read about it across as wide a spectrum of cultures, mythologies, religions, and experiences as possible.

This section offers an annotated list of readings you may wish to use toward enriching your own notions about spirituality. This list is not an exhaustive one; it simply offers a selection of possible launch points for a reading program that cannot other than be uniquely your own.

Indeed, it doesn't matter where any of us chooses to enter the stream. What matters is that we be willing to venture sufficiently far from shore such that the great current of change takes us where we need to go.

Armstrong, Karen. *A History of God: The 4,000-Year Quest of Judaism, Christianity and Islam.* **New York: Knopf, 1994.**
Written by a former Catholic nun, this ambitious book provides us with a perspective on mankind's pursuit for the "one right way" to think about God, and thereby the "true nature" of human spirituality, that we could not easily derive elsewhere, especially through a composite of accidental readings. This book is as valuable for providing us with insights into the essential needs and drives of human nature as it is in revealing certain

patterns that recur throughout the history of the human pursuit of the ultimate wellhead of meaning.

Brown, Joseph Eppes. *The Sacred Pipe*. **New York: Penguin, 1976.**

Based on the author's extensive interviews with Black Elk, former spiritual leader of the Oglala Sioux, this short book serves as an excellent introduction into Native American spirituality, which is well worth taking a close look at. After reading this book, you may be left wondering just who were the primitives, who the enlightened ones, when the White Man "conquered" the American West. Provides insight into universal spirituality (all things being of "spirit"), and into the renewing role of ritual.

Campbell, Joseph. *The Transformations of Myth Through Time*. **New York: Harper & Row, 1990**

Joseph Campbell's PBS series, *The Power of Myth*, with Bill Moyers, stirred something of a renaissance of interest in spirituality issues in America. Although Campbell is not one of the more lucid or focused writer/editors on spirituality issues, this overview on mythology (based on another, perhaps lesser known PBS series) is well worth reading. If nothing else, it will introduce you to the ascending chakras of kundalini yoga and leave you with a vivid picture of "big ferry boat" Buddhism versus "little ferry boat" Buddhism.

Eisler, Riane. *The Chalice and the Blade.* **New York: Harper & Row, 1987.**

This well-researched book builds a convincing case as the author illuminates the damage done to human aspiration and spiritual progress by 5000 years of what the author terms the "androcratic paradigm" (the "blade"). These hierarchical models of rule and control, Riane argues, have resulted in political, economic, and spiritual repression—especially of women—rather than in cooperation and "equalitarianism". This book may make you mad as hell, but I think you will find it ultimately liberating and healing.

Estés, Clarissa Pinkola, Ph.D. *Women Who Run With the Wolves*. New York: Ballentine Books, 1992.

If you are female and you need permission and guidance toward restoring your "wild woman" (the fullness of your authentic self), this book can be both empowering and inspirational. The author (a woman who is clearly that of which she speaks) draws a parallel between the fate of women and that of the oppressed wolf. Using a series of poignant myths and stories, Estés gently and gracefully leads you toward "singing over your bones" (reclaiming the fullness of your soul). Any man who loves a woman and realizes that real love is mutual soul-making should also read this book.

Fox, Matthew. *Original Blessing*. Sante Fe, NM: Bear & Co., 1983.

Anyone who feels maimed or abused at the hands of the concepts of "original sin" or sex as perversion may find liberation in this road map to "creation" spirituality. Fox, a former Dominican priest, is described as "a crusader and a smasher of chains". "What religion must let go of in the West," he writes, "is an exclusively fall/redemption model of spirituality."

Keen, Sam. *Hymns to an Unknown God: Awakening the Spirit in Everyday Life*. New York: Bantam, 1994.

This extended definition of human spirituality is a bit overwritten (as with a holograph, you have to look beyond all the swirls of surface color); however, if you are patient, there is fodder here for anyone who is on or about to embark on a journey of fundamental change. This book may be especially helpful to anyone who no longer holds organized religion as a source of spiritual sustenance and is looking for an alternative source that does not involve New-Age cults or pop-culture fads. This book offers more in the way of general exhortations than specific how-to guidance. (Hint: If you are impatient, begin on page 76, "Religion and the Spiritual Quest.")

Mitchell, Stephen, ed. *Tao Te Ching*. **New York:**
Harper & Row, 1988.
These philosophical lyrics were written by the Chinese
teacher/mystic Lao-tzu in the time of Confucius (at about the time
of the dawning of the Golden Age in Greece). They serve as a concise introduction into Eastern mysticism and spirituality. Women
especially may find the equal inclusion and celebration of the
female principle very refreshing. You may wish to read these
evocative lyrics more than once, over time.

Moore, Thomas. *Care of the Soul: A Guide for Cultivating Depth*
and Sacredness in Everyday Life. **New York: HarperCollins,**
1992.
This homeopathic approach to nurturing a needy soul reframes
symptoms as opportunities to move out of symptoms by moving
through them. In differentiating between "cure" and "care," it
advocates the efficacy of inaction (observing, reflecting, and imag-
ining) over perfective action (fixing, adjusting, and changing). The
differentiation between "cure" and "care" might be viewed as
building on the Bernie Siegel"s differentiation between "curing a
disease" and "healing a life" (see **Siegel, Bernie** below).
   Caution: Although this book purports to be a "guide," it is really more of an intellectual massage, likely to leave you feeling better in palpable but strangely vague ways but not likely to leave you
with a specific plan for tomorrow morning when the alarm goes
off. Also, in being heavily reliant on wringing conforming inter-
pretations from ancient myths, it may tend to be elusive, confusing, and even contradictory.

Pagels, Elaine. *Adam, Eve and the Serpent*. **New York:**
Random House, 1988.
   The author focuses on how the Augustinian interpretation of the
Adam and Eve story in the book of Genesis has affected our common culture and our individual conscience since the fourth cen-
tury C.E. Questions you may wish to bring to this book: Just what
is the creation story in the Old Testament trying to tell us about
human spirituality? How valid is this message?

Shealy, C. Norman, M.D., Ph.D. & Myss, Caroline M., M.A. *The Creation of Health: The Emotional, Psychological, and Spiritual Responses that Promote Health and Healing.* **Walpole, NH: Stillpoint Publishing, 1993.**

This book provides us with insights into the essential role our spiritual life plays in our overall health and well-being. A passage from Bernie S. Siegel's Foreword captures the essence: "The issue isn't to cure all illnesses. Everyone dies, someday. The issue is to love and live an *authentic life* (emphasis mine) and to understand that healing and curing may be two different entities."

Siegel, Bernie S., M.D. *Love, Medicine and Miracles.* **New York: Harper & Row, 1986.**

If you have always suspected there can be deeper dimensions to disease than merely catching a "bug" ("Why do you need this disease?"), and deeper dimensions to healing than merely taking a pill, you will likely find this book profoundly confirming and inspiring. The author, a Yale-educated surgeon, empowers us to use our natural powers of self-healing not so much to cure our physical illness, which is not always possible, but to heal our spiritual lives, which is always possible. "It's not how long you live that matters," he gently reminds us. "It's how you live in the moment."

Siegel, Bernie S, M.D. *Peace, Love and Healing.* **New York: Harper & Row, 1989.**

Subtitled "Bodymind Communication and the Path to Self healing: An Exploration," this is one of those rare sequels that is not only worth the bother but is perhaps even better than the original. A quote from the Introduction captures the essence: "When talking to . . . exceptional patients the words love, faith, living in the moment, forgiveness and hope come up again and again. *The inner peace these people have acquired on a psychospiritual level leads to healing* (emphasis added)."

In addition, I strongly recommend the essays of Lewis Thomas, especially those in his collections *The Lives of a Cell* and *The Medusa and the Snail.* I personally found Thomas' concise revelations on mutuality (symbiosis) and the degree of intricate (sometimes "mind-blowing") complexity and evolutionary ingenuity in the World of Living Things a wondrous and highly spiritual experience.

If you have not already seen it, I also recommend you watch Bill Moyers' six-part interview series with Joseph Campbell, titled *The Power of Myth*, or read the companion book of the same title.

Appendix B.
Footprints

Spirituality is like art: We can't really define it, but we all know when we are in its soul-filling presence. Likewise, we all know when we are not in its presence. For example, we sit in front of our television sets listening to yet another mechanically scripted, impeccably coifed piped piper tell us we can have it all if only we will elect *him* to office, instead of his dishonorable opponent. Even the most gullible among us senses we are hardly in the presence of unconditional selflessness. We know that the reach of the caring and concern we are witnessing extends little beyond our vote, not to mention our wallet. However, when we listen to people like Chief Seattle on the occasion of his being forced to "sell" land that, in his view, was inseparable from the very soul of his people, we know we are in a very different presence. We feel it on the most fundamental level of our being.

Sometimes it is useful for us to immerse ourselves in such presences, to fit our feet into the indelible footprints these presences leave behind, to walk a few steps in the same direction. If doing this accomplishes nothing else, it at least provides us with another possibility and another path to take. This appendix provides two sets of such footprints for us to follow to whatever extent possible. These two examples were chosen to suggest the universality of the deep notions underlying what we call spirituality. They also suggest the profound, soul-filling power of these notions. The first set of footprints is Chief Seattle's haunting plea; the second set is a simple tribute presented by two daughters at their father's memorial service.

The President in Washington sends word that he wishes to buy our land. But how can you buy or sell the sky, the land? The idea is strange to us. If we do not own the presence of the air and the sparkle of the water, how can you buy them? Every part of this earth is sacred to my people. Every shining pine needle. Every sandy shore. Every mist in the dark woods. Every meadow. Every humming insect. All are holy in the memory and experience of my people.

We know the sap that courses through the trees as we know the blood that courses through our veins. We are part of the earth and it is part of us. Perfumed flowers are our sisters. The bear, the deer, the great eagle, these are our brothers. The rocky crests, the juices in the meadow, the body heat of the pony, and man, all belong to the same family. The shining water that moves in the streams and rivers is not just water but the blood of our ancestors.

If we sell you our land you must remember that it is sacred. Each ghostly reflection in the clear water of the lakes tells of events and memories in the life of my people. The waters' murmur is the voice of my father's father. The rivers are our brothers. They quench our thirst. They carry our canoes and feed our children. So you must give to the rivers the kindness you would give any brother.

If we sell you our land, remember that the air is precious to us. That the air shares it spirit with all the life that it supports. The wind that gave our grandfather his first breath also receives his last sigh. The wind also gives our children the spirit of life. So if we sell you our land, you must keep it apart and sacred as a place where man can go to taste the wind that is sweetened by the meadow flowers.

Will you teach your children what we have taught our children, that the earth is our mother? What befalls earth befalls the sons of the earth. This we know. The earth does not belong to man. Man belongs to the earth. All things are connected like the blood that unites us all. Man did not weave the web of life, he is merely a strand in it. Whatever he does to the web he does to himself. One thing we know, our God is your God. The earth is precious to Him. And to harm the earth is to heap contempt on its creator.

Your destiny is a mystery to us. What will happen when the buffalo are all slaughtered? The wild horses tamed? What will happen when the secret corners of the forest are heavy with the scent of many men and the view of the ripe hills is blotted by talking wires? Where will the thicket be? Gone. Where will the eagle be? Gone. And what is it to say good-bye to the swift pony and the hunt? The end of living and the beginning of survival. When the last red man has vanished with his wilderness and his memory is only the shadow of a cloud moving across the prairie, will these shores and forests still be here? Will there be any of the spirit of my people left?

We love this earth as a newborn loves its mother's heartbeat. So, if we sell you our land, love it as we have loved it. Care for it as we have cared for it. Hold in your hand the memory of the land as it is when you receive it. Preserve the land for all children, and love it as God loves us all. As we are part of the land, you too are part of the land. This earth is precious to us, it is also precious to you.

One thing we know, there is only one God. No man, be he red man or white, can be apart. We are brothers, after all.

—Statement from Chief Seattle to Isaac Stevens
Governor of the Washington Territory, 1854

Stewart James Sandeman
March 13, 1916–October 24, 1986

We think of the earth, the living earth, as a single organism, with all living things, including us, being its myriad parts . . . its cells, so to speak. Each of us is independent, a separate living entity, yet each of us is dependent on all the rest. We cannot live one without the other.

On the surface of things, this may not always be obvious, and so it can be easy for us to depreciate our individual worth within the larger scheme of things. But if we look deeper, we quickly perceive that each individual is vital to the organic whole, the spiritual whole . . . and often in ways not easily analyzed, labeled, or quantified. None of us can live and grow, in any of the ways human beings can grow, without countless connections to others.

We each, moment-to-moment, toss pebbles into the pond of our common being, our common spirit, causing ripples of influence, sometimes perceptible, often not, to radiate outward, ultimately touching all on earth that lives.

Our father Stewart was a man whose life touched others quietly but deeply. He was a man who had no need to elevate himself above others. His gentleness and compassion extended not only to his family and friends, but also to the people who worked for him, and to anyone else he encountered. He was generous in spirit, sharing all that he had, and his sense of humor permeated his life, even up to the time of his death. His gift of music brought joy and pleasure to each of us who heard him sing, or sang with him, enriching our lives immeasurably. He was a man who quietly loved and communed with the other creatures who share this world with us; he especially loved the birds . . . .

That cardinal Dad fed cold winter-morning after cold winter-morning at the feeder he kept just outside his kitchen window may be the same cardinal who, next spring, sits at the very top of your highest tree, singing his heart out, celebrating the birth of the next generation . . . the continuation of the miracle of our common being.

St. Paul's Church
Wickford, Rhode Island
October 28, 1986

Appendix C.
Finding the Right
Therapist

When we need to rely on the services of a "healer"—a physician, a therapist—many of us have a tendency to invest our trust too quickly and too completely. We tend to subordinate ourselves to these "larger" people just as children tend to subordinate themselves to adults, and to view them as being almost godlike in their knowledge and power, as being all-loving caregivers who will always have our best interests at heart, no matter what. Unfortunately, we live in a world in which this childlike attitude can get us into a great deal of trouble.

The problem is that too many of these caregivers do not in fact have our best interests at heart. Too many therapists are in the "business" to make money and/or gain prestige, to exercise unchallenged power and authority over others, to shield themselves from having to deal with their own dysfunction (better to tell others how to deal with theirs), or to prey on the weak and the vulnerable in order to feed their own sickness.

Despite this disappointing reality, however, it is not the whole reality; there are indeed many competent, compassionate therapists. A sufficient number, certainly, for us to be able to find one who will work for us (in both senses of the phrase).

This appendix offers some specific guidelines intended to help you find a therapist who is *properly trained* to address your specific needs, who is a *true caregiver* (rather than a bottom-line businessperson), and who adheres to the highest standards of *ethical* behavior. Too much is at stake for you not to take at least a minimal number of precautions.

• Do your homework.

Psychotherapy is an inexact science. In fact, it is not really a science at all; it is an amalgam of science, art, and pure, unadulterated "magic." For this reason, it tends to be a welcoming place for what can be perceived as a bewildering, if not overwhelming, host of theories, philosophies, mindsets, opinions, biases, orientations, methodologies, and styles. On one extreme, there is the analytical, reductionist approach that is characteristic of the traditional "medical model'; on the other, the holistic, inclusionary approach that is characteristic of the "systems model." There is the leisurely approach that dwells on the problem (exhuming it from the deep, dark catacombs of our psyche); the more focused approach that dwells on the solution (finding one that "works'). There is the approach that differentiates "normal" from "abnormal" (or "functional" from "dysfunctional'). There is the nonpathologizing approach that views all states of being as value-neutral points on a continuum. And, of course, there's everything in between. (Want to get "better?" Then move your point on the curve of "happiness."

To find the right practitioner, therefore, we must determine which of all these alternative approaches is likely to work best for us, taking into consideration who we are, what we believe, how we operate, and how we think. In other words, we need to do a little research. For example, we might wish to visit the local library or bookstore to get a cross-section of reference literature on psychotherapy, and we might wish to talk with friends or acquaintances (more than one) who have had firsthand experience with some form of psychotherapy. We might even wish to visit a public mental-health facility to ask basic questions of the professional staff (while noting how we are treated there, as a human being). In other words, we need to do sufficient research such that the multiple-choice quiz. we deliver gives us the results we need to take the best care of ourselves.

The level of satisfaction we receive at a restaurant depends not so much on the kind of cuisine the restaurant specializes in as it does on the particular chef who prepares it. So too does the satisfaction we receive from psychotherapy depend more on the particular caregiver—who this person is as a human being, what his or her personal "magic"—than on theoretical orientation.

The key question is always not "What is your theory?", but "Why are you in this 'business' anyway?"

• **Narrow the field.**

To prevent ourselves from becoming overwhelmed, we need to narrow the field of possibilities to a manageable level as quickly as possible. We can do this by applying certain key criteria to whatever set of possibilities we find open to us. As a practical matter, the pre-eminent of these key criteria may well be the kind of credentials our insurance company will pay for (only Ph.D.'s and M.D.'s, for example, in which case our search field quickly becomes narrowed to clinical psychologists and psychiatrists).

Perhaps the next most important criterion to apply is the therapeutic orientation, or approach, we have decided on; however, we may wish to remain somewhat flexible on this one, for the reason stated above: The right person can be more crucial than the right theory. Another criterion some of us may wish to apply is gender. If we are female, for example, and we have a history of being sexually abused, we may wish to consider only female candidates, for obvious reasons. Similarly, if we are gay or lesbian, we may wish to consider only candidates who are homosexual, or who at least have a history of working with gay or lesbian clients.

Another limiting criterion we may wish to consider is the ethnic or cultural background of the candidates. For example, if we are black and Muslim, or Native American and "traditional," we may wish to avoid candidates who are white and orthodox Jewish, or white and fundamentalist Christian. Not because there is anything inherently "wrong" with these candidates (because of what or who they are), but because fundamental differences in culture, experience, and/or beliefs can impose invisible barriers that can impede the therapeutic process.

In short, consider applying whatever criteria you, as a unique, sovereign individual, feel you need to apply in order to feel safe and comfortable with a person in whom you are about to invest more trust than you likely have invested in anyone in your memorable lifetime.

One size does not fit all—never has, never will.

- **Ask for recommendations from others, but be wary.**

Asking recommendations from others is always fraught with danger, for several reasons:

1. People's knowledge is necessarily limited to what they have experienced.

2. People tend to be reluctant to admit mistakes.

3. People tend to like to take on the role of "an authority," even when the basis for such authority is a bit thin. (As Andy Warhol put it, "Everybody will be famous for fifteen minutes.") Have you ever met anyone who was reluctant to recommend the car they were driving (even though it just came out of the shop—again)?

However, individual experience is still a good source of valuable information, especially if we use it as a starting point, a manageable way to begin. Other people's experience is not necessarily wisdom, but we can make it so, simply by challenging every recommendation with a few gentle, but probing questions; for example:

— How did you decide on this person?

— How long have you been seeing this person?

— What is the goal of your therapy?

— How does this person interact with you?

— What do you like best about this person's approach? What least?

— What has been most helpful (and least helpful) about your work with this person?

Remember: Most bad decisions are not the result of bad judgment, but of good judgment being applied to bad or insufficient information.

- **Be your own advocate.**

Now comes the hard part, at least for a great many of us: Confronting the "authority figure" directly—head on. Risking conflict. Risking rejection. Risking the consequences of taking care of ourselves.

We have done our homework; we have narrowed our list to perhaps three to five candidates; it's now time to interview each one of these candidates, either on the telephone or in an initial visit (which should be at no charge, by the way; if it isn't, this is all the information you will need).

Before you call or visit any of the candidates on your list, however, prepare a brief list of questions, as a way both of focusing your interview and of ensuring you come away from it with all the information you intended to get; it's easy for us to get distracted, especially when our primary interest is really to "get the damn thing over with".

We don't need to play "Twenty Questions." A few key questions should be sufficient. For example:

— What is your education and training?

— What licenses do you hold?

— How did you happen to choose this line of work?

— What is your current case load?

— What is your therapeutic orientation? What models do you use?

— What characteristics would you look for in a therapist for yourself?

— How do you stay current in the field?

Listen to the answers, and ask follow-up questions as they occur to you; but also tune into the intangibles: tone of voice (any defensiveness, impatience, condescension?), repeated interruptions, and (if you visit) body language, eye contact, look in the eyes, number of times a timepiece is scanned, etc.

In other words, be your own advocate. You are not only purchasing a life-critical service; you are investing your precious trust. You are placing your vulnerability wholly in the hands of another human being, an "authority figure" of great power, realizing that if you do not wholly trust this person, all will be for naught.

The first step in asking others to stand up for us is to stand up for ourselves.

- **Beware of any practitioner who promises an easy path to Nirvana.**

We are all genetically predisposed toward laziness. We'd rather spend fifteen minutes driving around the mall parking lot than spend an extra two minutes walking an extra fifty yards from a more-distance parking space. And we all buy the diet book that tells us we can have our cake and eat it too, rather than the one that tells us in order to lose weight *and keep it off* we must completely redefine our relationship to food. Besides just costing us needless time, though, this natural predisposition, greatly magnified in some of us, can get us into trouble. It can lead us deeper into an already existing spiral of failure. It can place us in the hands of charlatans and predators. It can sap energy and resources we can never recover to use to do our real work.

Rule of Thumb: Change that is truly fundamental in its reach is NEVER EASY and NEVER SHORT. Remedies such as Eye Movement Desensitizing and Reprocessing Therapy may indeed be useful, but they are not likely to change our life.

No pain, no gain.

Glossary

The purpose of this glossary is to clarify how various key terms are intended to be used in this guide book. The terms are listed in alphabetical order except where certain related terms are grouped together, as in the first entry below:

Anger/Rage/Hate

The term anger denotes a powerful, transforming, potentially dominating emotion that allows us to objectify those people (including "'intimates'") who either threaten us or cause us harm. Evolved and biologically reinforced over the eons, anger is a value-neutral (neither inherently "good" nor inherently "bad') defense mechanism that, like the adrenaline it releases, paves the way for aggressive, self-preserving behavior.

When we are able to objectify someone—to perceive this person as an abstraction ("threat'," "'enemy") rather than as a sentient, kindred being—we are released, at least in part, from the normal behavior constraints that would otherwise be placed on us by our natural inclinations toward compassion and cooperation. Thus freed, we can then lash out either to defend ourselves or to avenge ourselves. Anger is the magic that transforms the Dr. Jekyll in us into the Mr. Hyde we are all capable of being.

Anger, and the "'fight'" behaviors it triggers, usually comes into play when our first line of defense, fear, and the "'flight'" response it triggers, is not, or is no longer, an option.

Rage is anger elevated, accumulated, multiplied. Rage frees us to defend ourselves to any extreme (often to the point of regret).

Hate is unresolved anger—the pus of festering, unattended wounds, the gangrene of a poisoned soul.

Body Mind/Spirit Mind

Body mind is that part of our consciousness that governs our secular, or ego, self (see below). Its primary concern is the preservation and well-being of our physical self, or, in other words, bringing us the kind of happiness (comfort, pleasure, security) that is predominantly of a physical dimension. **Spirit mind,** on the other hand, is that part of our consciousness that governs our spiritual self. Its primary concern is bringing us the kind of happiness (fulfillment, inner peace, harmony) that is predominantly of a spiritual dimension. Whereas body mind attempts to fulfill its mission by focusing our attention and energy on accumulating the kind of practical knowledge and understanding that translates into some form of secular happiness, spirit mind attempts to fulfill its mission by focusing our attention and energy on accumulating the kind of wisdom and enlightenment that translates into personal fulfillment.

For example, when body mind contemplates a forest of old-growth trees, it reasons: This forest is separate from me; it is of lesser importance than am I. This forest represents millions of board-feet of lumber, which in turn represents many millions of dollars, of which I am in need of an unlimited quantity, to meet my unlimited needs. I will devise efficient ways to take of this forest all that I can (or can get away with).

When spirit mind contemplates the same forest, it reasons: This forest and I are essential parts of the same whole; in the eyes of our common Source we are brothers in spirit, complements in purpose. My responsibility toward this forest, as toward all kindred others, is to honor and reverence the full expression of its being, to protect it from all harm, by me or by others, that would threaten the well-being of the Greater Whole.

Ideally, the unmitigated tension between these two viewpoints brings about a natural balance—that is, the absence of excess in any direction. For example, the body mind and the spirit mind that each contemplate a forest of old-growth trees may resolve the extremes of their respective viewpoints into the following synthesis: We will take of this forest no more than we require to meet our need for a reasonable level of physical comfort and well-being; we will give back to this forest all that it should require to replenish and evolve itself, both for its own sake and for that of all those who are to follow us. We hold the beauty of this forest in reverence and in awe.

Unfortunately, in our culture, which has become almost thoroughly secularized, this kind of natural balance is rarely achieved.

Ego Self/Secular Self

This guide book takes the view that our humanness is of two dimensions: the secular (bounded), and the spiritual (unbounded). The term **ego self** is meant to denote our secular, bounded dimension, that is, everything about us that has to do with our separateness, and with the self-consciousness and self-absorption that our separateness tends naturally to impose upon us.

Our ego self is our self-preservation self, our "get our share" self, our "what's in it for me" self, our accumulating self. It is the gravitational center of all our self-directed (versus other-directed) instincts, wants, desires, and cravings, pulling into itself whatever it "needs." Left unmodulated, this gravitational center can readily grow in mass to the point of collapsing into a "black hole," locking within itself even the faintest glimmer of the light of the other essential dimension of our self: our giving self, spiritual self. It can become so massively focused on itself, in fact, on its "neediness," that serving it becomes our only meaning; we become virtually its prisoner—alienated from all else.

From the perspective of the ego self, "progress" and "growth" are essentially material in nature; they encompass whatever adds a measure of safety and security, whatever makes us feel less vulnerable, whatever provides a modicum of freedom from the tyranny of all those forces out there, real or imagined, that would do us harm.

In this guide book, ego self is used interchangeably with **secular self.**

Guilt

The term **guilt** as used in this guide book is intended to denote another of the evolved, value-neutral defense mechanisms

Nature uses to help ensure our survival and well-being. Guilt functions to regulate our behavior by alerting us when our behavior toward other members of our essential communities (family, friends, clan, tribe) is of such a nature as to threaten us with expulsion or separation from these essential communities. Guilt is a warning.

As in the case of anger and shame, if guilt is allowed to accumulate over time and is not resolved in some way (through atonement, reconciliation, or change in behavior), it can build in size and power until, at some point, it essentially takes control of us and defines us in its own image.

Healing/Recovery

Used figuratively, physical **healing** can be a powerful metaphor, triggering images of flesh magically regenerating itself and bones miraculously fusing themselves. Healing may evoke strong, positive feelings of hope, renewal, and self-empowerment. However, as in the case of all metaphors, images of physical healing can be overused (even to the point of losing their power), and they can be used inappropriately—even misleadingly. Physical healing is not necessarily the appropriate metaphor to use in all situations involving some kind of "injury."

This guide book takes the view that images of physical healing can sometimes be counterproductive when applied to "healing" the emotional and spiritual injuries of family dysfunction, especially the more extreme forms of such dysfunction. The problem is that in this particular context the physical (mechanical) model of healing tends to focus our attentions and energies on trying to recover lost states of being (e.g., the "lost" child of our lost childhood) that simply never can be recovered. It also tends to imply a reliance on external remedies and interventions (magical cures) as opposed to internal resources and personal responsibility (hard work).

In this guide book, the term healing (as well as the term **recovery**) is meant to denote a sense of releasing and moving beyond our losses—pulling ourselves out of a mire of "stuckness"—rather than regenerating a previous state of being or reclaiming something that has been unfairly taken from us. Although this difference may be subtle, it is always fundamental.

Self-esteem

Self-esteem is the quality of knowing we are inherently lovable and unconditionally worthy of love, respect, and acceptance. Being self-esteeming is being comfortable with ourselves "just the way we are". Though self-esteem may seem almost synonymous with *self-confidence*, the two are really very different (as in the case of guilt and shame). Whereas our self-esteem concerns how lovable we feel we are, our self-confidence concerns how skillful or knowledgeable we feel we are. Our self-esteem derives from the simple knowledge that we harbor deep within us a timeless, undiminishable spark of the eternal, the great mystery, the "divine'; our self-confidence derives from the measure of our successes on the various battlefields of life. One is purely spiritual in nature, the other purely secular.

Narcissism and arrogance derive not from an overdose self-esteem but from self-confidence gone awry, self-confidence transmuted into self-importance (common in Washington, D.C., for example, in the form of "Potomac fever'). In fact, it is a lack of self-esteem that drives us to take the path to narcissism and self-grandiosity. A lack of self-esteem creates a hunger that many of us misinterpret as a need for secular competence rather than spiritual sustenance

Self-esteem should be the prime concern of those of us who are parents. By loving our children without condition or personal agenda, we instill in them the bedrock on which they can construct a life truly worth living. Self-esteem is the greatest of all possible gifts.

Shame

Shame is another emotion (like guilt) that Nature has evolved over the kindred generations for the purpose of controlling our behavior. Shame pushes us very strongly toward correcting or altering our behavior for our own good and the good of the larger community. Though shame is seemingly very similar to guilt, it is really quite different: Whereas guilt is a voice that tells us *our behavior* was flawed *(it* had a negative effect on others), shame is a voice that tells us *we* are flawed *(we,* or at least a part of us, is having a negative effect on others). Guilt focuses us on our actions; shame on ourselves. Guilt is an internal response to a judgment we pass on ourselves; shame is an internal response to a judgment others pass, have passed, or might pass on us. Guilt punishes us with anguish, shame with humiliation.

Indeed, whereas guilt is the sting of the honey bee, shame is the sting of the scorpion. Shame, in other words, is strong medicine. But it (or something like it) has to be. Without it, or something equally as potent, the level of mutual trust and cooperation upon which depends our very survival as highly interdependent (but almost equally selfish) creatures would not be possible.

However, as in the case of all strong measures, shame is fraught with danger: Too much shame or shame made unresolvable (e.g., you are told, and come to believe, you are not lovable), can easily trigger a festering, self-perpetuating self-loathing so strong it causes the spiritual self, the "healing" self, to cannibalistically consume itself.

Spiritual/Spirituality

Those of us who have been thoroughly steeped in the flavor and stain of one of the various Judeo-Christian "teas" tend to take a very narrow view of what the terms **spiritual** and **spirituality** denote. Asked to play the word association game around these terms, the vast majority of us would come up with such coordinates as "religious," "God," "Bible," "Christ," "priest," "rabbi," "Mother Teresa," and "church." Others of us, pretending to higher ground, might come up with "born again," "moonie," "New Age," "Zen Buddhist," and "Hare Krishna"; but our view would be no less narrow. Very few of us would tend to associate, even with conscious forethought, such coordinates as "oneness," "connectedness," "wonder," "selflessness," "mystery," "compassion," or "unconditional love."

We of the Judeo-Christian tradition tend to limit our concept of what it means to be spiritual to the notion of being in a state of good standing with an aloof, paternalistic deity, one capable of punishing his "children," not merely by banishing them to their bedrooms for a few hours of self-reflection, but by locking them in the "basement" for an eternity of unimaginable horrors. To become spiritual, we must appease or win the favor of this stern and vindictive father figure through unquestioning obedience and unrestrained ingratiation. We demonstrate our obedience by strictly complying to "his will," as revealed in "sacred" scripture and "inspired" texts; we demonstrate our ingratiation by ritualistically subordinating ourselves: bowing, kneeling, genuflecting, thumping our breast.

Our focus, needless to say, tends to be on this exacting father figure, and on ourselves, rather than on each other.

Some of us have rejected this narrow view of spirituality, either consciously or by default. However, either because we are too busy doing other things (pursuing other "gods") or because we simply don't feel the need, we have largely neglected to fill the vacuum that our rejection has created. We may still go through the motions, attending church services on occasion, choosing to have our children baptized (just in case), observing the Christmas or Chanukah traditions; but our hearts and souls are simply not riding on the same bus with our actions. Our spirituality, then, is at most a minor aspect of our lives, one that requires that we make consciously-deliberate decisions about when, where, and how to address or pursue it (for example, whether to attend church this Sunday or stay home and read the Sunday paper over a cup of brewed coffee).

In the Judeo-Christian tradition, our spirituality is the degree to which we subordinate and diminish the self, the degree to which we become self-conscious and anxious under the steady gaze of a fearsome and demanding Judge, the degree to which we open our inherent darkness to the rays of Eternal Light—before it's too late. In this guide book, our spirituality is the extent to which we have been able to move away from the gravitational pull of our ego self—including away from the fierce hold that our fear and anger have over us—and to move toward unconditional acceptance and compassion, toward unself-conscious giving and sharing, toward unrestrained connection and kinship with all that is.

Our spirituality is the degree to which we expand our individuality and share it with all else, the degree to which we empty ourselves of fear and anxiety, the degree to which we allow the Eternal Light already within us to shine freely forth. (For a list of suggested readings on spirituality, refer to Appendix A.)

Spiritual Self

Our ego self is that part of our intrinsically dual self that makes us separate and bounded, individual. Our **spiritual self**, on the other hand, is that part of our dual self that makes us integral and boundless, one with all else—kindred with all else. It is that elusive, mysterious essence that transcends the mere sum of our biological parts; that makes us an essential part of the great mystery of creation; that gives us true and lasting meaning; that makes us equal in the "eyes" of the whole; that gives us all the reason we will ever need to be reverent toward ourselves, toward all others, toward all else.

Whereas our ego self is governed by our **body mind** and is primarily motivated by concerns of self-preservation, and is therefore focused on getting and accumulating, our spiritual self is governed by our **spirit mind** and is motivated by concerns of fulfillment. It is focused on giving and sharing. It is our "how can I be of help" self, our "how can I make things better" self, our "how can I make a difference" self. It is the part of our dual self that has the capacity to extend love and compassion unconditionally—to ourselves as well as to all others.

Our spiritual self is our connection with, our participation in, the eternal. It is not only the source of all meaning, it is meaning itself. If our soul is the chrysalis of our potential to discover and to be truth, to create and to be beauty, to attain and to be harmony, to build and to be wholeness—then our spiritual self is the butterfly that emerges.

(For examples of the kind of indelible "footprints" that the spiritual self leaves behind, refer to Appendix B.)

Truth

In the West we tend to believe that all **truth** is external, that the fundamental principles and truths we need to guide our lives toward happiness and fulfillment are accessible and knowable only through some external source. We tend, therefore, to seek guidance in our parents, teachers, elders, canon texts, pop culture, leaders, heroes and role models, experts and specialists, celebrities, sacred scriptures, and, alas, the self-help aisle at our local bookstores. Few of us seek fundamental guidance within ourselves. And yet very few of us would not ultimately come to agree, if we were to take sufficient time out from the clutter and clamor of our harried lives to think about it, that all the truth any of us needs to know in order to live a fulfilling life, will ever need, lies written plainly within the sacred core of every human being.

Indeed, this guide book takes the view that each one of us is delivered into this world not only with all the "hardware" and "software" components we need in order to fulfill our purpose, and therefore ourselves, but with the complete user manual as well, a full set of instructions that, unlike those that come with our VCRs and all those other gadgets that complicate and confound our lives, is clearly and unambiguously composed. Every "spiritual" truth we will ever need to know is fully accessible to every one of us who will but take the trouble to open the golden cover of the oracle within and scan its indelibly inscribed pages. If we need external interventions (experts) for anything, this guide book holds, we need them only to remind us of what we already "know'—to perhaps lead us to the wellspring of our own ageless wisdom so that we might then freely drink.

Victimhood

The term **victimhood**, as used in this guide book, is intended to denote a state of being in which victims of childhood trauma have become so strongly focused on healing the particular ways in which they have been wounded or damaged, or on recovering what has been lost or taken away from them, that the process toward healing has tended to become more important than the healing itself.

Victimhood is characterized by strongly identifying oneself as a victim (ACOA, survivor, codependent), sometimes to the point of pride; by tending to dwell on the past, often narrowly on certain events in the past; by finding oneself seemingly trapped in a recursive cycle of rage (other-blaming) and despair (self-blaming); and by moving from one unsatisfying remedy to another (shifting one's "secular center" from here to there, hither and yon).

Victimhood is a state of inertia, of stuckness, of plateauing—of being bound by that which one is hanging on to. Victimhood is a battered soul wearing permanent disability plates.

Wounded Child

Much of the popular literature on recovering from childhood trauma takes the view that there is within us a **wounded child**, huddling in the shadows of our maimed and scarred soul, and that we must "heal" this wounded child in order to recover from the terrible effects of the trauma we suffered; we must, in effect, become for ourselves the parents we never had when we most needed them.

This guide book takes the view that there is an unresolved *loss* within us, the loss of a entire childhood, and that we must acknowledge, mourn, and let go of this loss if we are truly to "get on with it." There comes a point in our recovery process, this guide book assumes, when we must recognize that we can never recover what has been irretrievably lost, and that if we are to get past the pain and anger that is binding us to an unhappy past, including to all the players who made it so, we must focus our energies on becoming the whole, glorious, functional, contributory, magnificent adult we were meant to be.

To laugh often and much; to win the respect of intelligent people and the affection of children; to earn the appreciation of honest critics and endure the betrayal of false friends; to appreciate beauty, to find the best in others; to leave the world a bit better, whether by a healthy child, a garden patch or a redeemed social condition; to know even one life has breathed easier because you have lived.
This is to have succeeded.
—Ralph Waldo Emerson

Life is the game that must be played:
This truth at least, good friends, we know;
So live and laugh, nor be dismayed
As one by one the phantoms go.
—Edwin Arlington Robinson,
Ballade by the Fire

About the Author

Finding himself in middle age alternately raging at a deceased father who left him feeling unlovable and plummeting into ever-deeper depths of despair, Tom Fitzgerald eventually entered what has become the canon path to "recovering" from the insidious effects of having grown up in an alcoholic family: volumes of reading, hours of individual and family psychotherapy, weekly twelve-step meetings, John Bradshaw, Joseph Campbell, aerobics, running marathons, vitamin pills, health spas, journaling, nurturing the "inner child." Although most of these therapies proved helpful, they also seemed to become an end unto themselves. Tom began to sense, both in himself and in others, that recovery was becoming not only a state of being ("I'm an ACoA and damned proud of it."), but also a state of mind. ("I'm a 'wounded child.' " "I'm a victim.") Ultimately feeling a need to "get on with it," to move beyond the preoccupations of his wounded ego self, Tom stepped outside his circle of recovery and took a good look at his life, at where he was headed (and not headed), and then launched himself down a path toward realizing what he had come to believe was perhaps the only paradise *any* of us can ever attain: knowing at the moment of our death we have lived an authentic life, that we have left behind more than we have taken, that we have chosen not to consume our precious lives trying, in various futile ways, to recover what can never be recovered. The process he used to move himself down this path is the basis of this book.

Tom has spoken on the spiritual dimension of recovery and wellness at conferences, and has conducted workshops based on the "greening the garden within" paradigm presented in this guide book.

Author of three novels and one other nonfiction work, Tom Fitzgerald also helped author three sons, now grown and graduated from college.

He served as a Navy SEAL during the Vietnam War. Holder of degrees in mathematics, industrial management, and English, Fitzgerald has been a college instructor, a vocational & life skills counselor for retarded children and adults, a door-to-door salesman of home-study courses, a stockbroker, the assistant to the president of a large health-care corporation, a Washington lobbyist, the PR writer for a New England school district, a technical writer, a corporate manager, and a private consultant. He has swum across Lake Ontario, jumped out of planes and helicopters with a piece of silk on his back, and run the Boston Marathon three times. He lives in seacoast New Hampshire with his wife of twenty-eight years, two cats, and a bird.